BUILDING BASIC VOCABULARY C

Robert J. Marzano

NATIONAL GEOGRAPHIC LEARNING | CENGAGE Learning·

Australia • Brazil • Japan • Korea • Mexico • Singapore • Spain • United Kingdom • United States

Building Basic Vocabulary C
Robert J. Marzano

Publisher: Sherrise Roehr

Executive Editor: Carmela Fazzino-Farah

Managing Editor: Kellie Cardone

Development Editors: Cécile Engeln and Marissa Petrarca

Senior Product Manager: Barbara Quincer Coulter

Associate Marketing Manager: Jennifer Ellegood

Director of Content and Media Production: Michael Burggren

Senior Content Project Manager: Daisy Sosa

Manufacturing Manager: Marcia Locke

Manufacturing Buyer: Marybeth Hennebury

Cover Design: Page 2 LLC

Interior Design: Muse Group, Inc.

Composition: PreMediaGlobal

Contributing Writers: Karen Haller Beer, Jackie Counts, and Wendy Criner

ISBN-13: 978-1-133-31649-7

ISBN-10: 1-133-31649-2

National Geographic Learning
20 Channel Center St.
Boston, MA 02210
USA

Cengage Learning is a leading provider of customized learning solutions with office locations around the globe, including Singapore, the United Kingdom, Australia, Mexico, Brazil, and Japan. Locate your local office at: **international.cengage.com/region**

Cengage Learning products are represented in Canada by Nelson Education, Ltd.

Visit National Geographic Learning online at **ngl.cengage.com**
Visit our corporate website at **www.cengage.com**

Printed in the United States of America
1 2 3 4 5 6 7 16 15 14 13 12

Renee M. Belvis
Dunedin Highland Middle
School
Dunedin, FL

Brian Cerda
Sabina Magnet School
Chicago, IL

Ashley Cimo
Amos Alonzo Stagg High
School
Palos Hills, IL

Fred Cochran
Lincoln Unified School District
Stockton, CA

Raquel Cruz
Country Club Middle School
Miami, FL

Meg Daniewicz
New Millennium Academy
Minneapolis, MN

Amber Driscoll
March Middle School
Moreno Valley, CA

Annie Duong
San Joaquin COE
Stockton, CA

Jill Hoffmann
Victor J. Andrew High School
Tinley Park, IL

Laura Hook
Howard County Public School
System
Ellicott City, MD

Tara Kim
March Middle School
Moreno Valley, CA

Alice Kos
Minneapolis Public Schools
Minneapolis, MN

Elizabeth Koutny
Ames Middle School
Berwyn, IL

Mary Lein
Rochester ISD
Rochester, MN

Sam Nofziger
The English Learner Group
Fresno, CA

Esmeralda Placencia
Chicago Public Schools
Chicago, IL

Maria Rivera
Richard Edwards Elementary
School
Chicago, IL

Mytzy Rodriguez-Kufner
Round Lake Area Schools
Round Lake, IL

Nathalie Rumowicz
Seminole Middle School
Plantation, FL

Susan Sharko
Old Quarry Middle School
Lemont, IL

Dr. LaWanna Shelton
Trevecca Nazarene University
Nashville, TN

Gwen Snow
Jefferson County Public Schools –
ESL Newcomer Academy
Louisville, KY

Claudia Viloria
South Ft. Myers High School
Ft. Myers, FL

Brenda Ward
Lafayette School Corporation
Lafayette, IN

Bryn Watson
Hough Street Elementary
School
Barrington, IL

Jennifer White
ESOL Program, Charleston
County School District
Charleston, SC

Vicki Writsel
Bowling Green Independent
Schools
Bowling Green, KY

CONTENTS

Book A Super Clusters

Book B Super Clusters

Book C Super Clusters

Note: This Contents section provides information on how to find the first instance of each super cluster. For information on where specific <u>clusters</u> can be found, please refer to the Appendix on pages 293 to 296.

166. Mathematical Operations

Check (✔) the words you already know. Then, listen and repeat.

Tracks 1–12

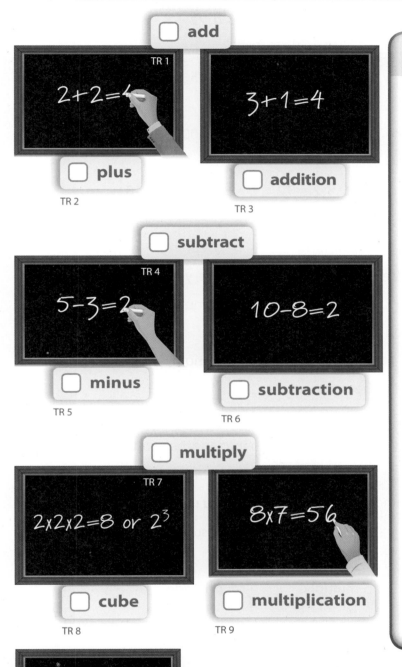

☐ add

TR 1

$2+2=4$

$3+1=4$

☐ plus

TR 2

☐ addition

TR 3

☐ subtract

TR 4

$5-3=2$

$10-8=2$

☐ minus

TR 5

☐ subtraction

TR 6

☐ multiply

TR 7

$2 \times 2 \times 2 = 8$ or 2^3

$8 \times 7 = 56$

☐ cube

TR 8

☐ multiplication

TR 9

$6 \div 2 = 3$

☐ divide

TR 10

☐ division

TR 11

Definitions

If you **add** numbers or amounts together, you calculate their total.

Addition is the process of calculating the total of two or more numbers.

If you **count** all the things in a group, you see how many there are.

When you **cube** a number, you multiply it by itself two times.

If you **divide** one number by another number, you find how many times the second number can fit into the first number.

Division is the process of dividing one number by another.

You use **minus** to take one number away from another number.

Multiplication is the process of adding a number to itself a certain number of times.

If you **multiply** a number, you add it to itself a certain number of times.

You use **plus** to show that you are adding one number to another number.

If you **subtract** one number from another, you take it away from the other number.

Subtraction is the act of taking one number away from another.

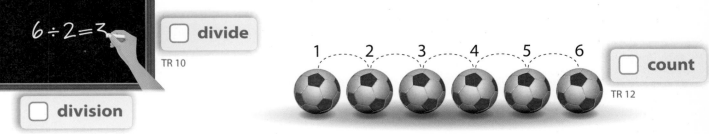

1   2   3   4   5   6

☐ count

TR 12

Check Your Understanding

A. Circle the correct answer.

1. An example of an *addition* problem is _____.

   a. $22 + 1 = 23$ b. $22 - 1 = 21$ c. $22 \times 1 = 22$ d. $22 \div 1 = 22$

2. An example of a *subtraction* problem is _____.

   a. $15 + 3 = 18$ b. $15 - 3 = 12$ c. $15 \times 3 = 45$ d. $15 \div 3 = 5$

3. An example of a *division* problem is _____.

   a. $100 + 2 = 102$ b. $100 - 2 = 98$ c. $100 \times 2 = 200$ d. $100 \div 2 = 50$

4. An example of a *multiplication* problem is _____.

   a. $36 + 2 = 38$ b. $36 - 2 = 34$ c. $36 \times 2 = 72$ d. $36 \div 2 = 18$

5. Which word describes this equation? $5^3 = 125$

   a. dividing   b. subtracting   c. counting   d. cubing

6. When you take a number and add it to itself a certain number of times, you are _____.

   a. adding   b. subtracting   c. dividing   d. multiplying

7. When you put two numbers together, you are _____.

   a. adding   b. subtracting   c. dividing   d. multiplying

8. When you take one number away from another, you are _____.

   a. adding   b. subtracting   c. dividing   d. multiplying

9. When you take one number and see how many times it can go into another, you are _____.

   a. adding   b. subtracting   c. dividing   d. multiplying

10. When you want to find out how many things there are in a group, you must _____.

    a. cube   b. count   c. divide   d. subtract

11. You use *minus* when you _____.

    a. add   b. subtract   c. multiply   d. divide

12. You use *plus* when you _____.

    a. add   b. subtract   c. multiply   d. divide

B. Write the words from the box in the correct column.

add	plus	cube	multiply
count	subtract	divide	subtraction
minus	addition	division	multiplication

WORDS RELATED TO PUTTING NUMBERS TOGETHER	WORDS RELATED TO BREAKING NUMBERS APART

Challenge Words

Check (✔) the words you already know.

☐ divisible   ☐ per   ☐ tally   ☐ times

340. Mathematical Quantities

Check (✔) the words you already know. Then, listen and repeat.

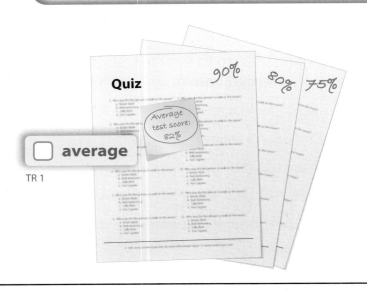

Quiz

Average test score: 82%

90% 80% 75%

□ average

TR 1

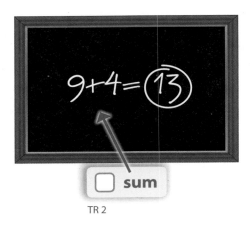

$9+4=\boxed{13}$

□ sum

TR 2

Check Your Understanding

A. Circle the correct answer to each question.

1. Which equation shows an average?

   a. $10 + 2 + 14 = 26$

   b. $10 + 2 + 14 = 26 \div 2 = 13$

   c. $10 + 12 + 4 + 2 = 28 \div 4 = 7$

   d. $10 + 12 + 14 = 36 \div 6 = 6$

2. Which equation shows a sum?

   a. $150 \div 2 = 75$

   b. $80 \times 4 = 320$

   c. $90 + 5 = 95$

   d. $500 - 350 = 150$

3. How can you find out the total number of students in a school?

   a. by subtracting the number of students from the number of teachers

   b. by adding together the number of students in each class

   c. by multiplying the number of students in each class by two

   d. by dividing the total number of classes

Johnny's Supermarket

Wheat bread	$3.59
Cheddar cheese	$4.00
Apples	$2.99
Oranges	$2.99
TOTAL	$13.57

☐ **total**

TR 3

Definitions

An **average** is the number found by adding all items in a group, such as test scores, and then dividing the scores by the number of tests in the group.

In mathematics, the **sum** is the total amount that results from adding two or more numbers together.

The **total** is the number that you get when you add several numbers together.

B. Write **T** for **true statements** and **F** for **false statements**.

1. _____ The sum of an addition problem is the same as the total.

2. _____ To find the average number of hours that you sleep in one week, you should add the number of hours you sleep each night and divide by seven.

3. _____ To find a sum, you subtract one or more numbers.

Challenge Words

Check (✔) the words you already know.

☐ area   ☐ maximum   ☐ multiple   ☐ proportion

☐ fraction   ☐ minimum   ☐ percent   ☐ ratio

410. Branches of Mathematics

Check (✔) the word if you already know it. Then, listen and repeat.

Track 1

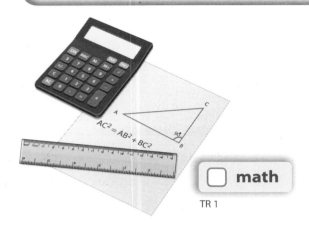

AC² = AB² + BC²

TR 1

☐ **math**

Definition

Math or **mathematics** is the study of numbers, quantities, or shapes.

Check Your Understanding

A. Look at the list of activities below. Check (✔) each one that requires **math**.

☐ reading a novel

☐ following a recipe

☐ sleeping

☐ shopping

☐ building a doghouse

B. Write **T** for **true statements** and **F** for **false statements**.

1. _____ When you multiply two numbers together, you are using math.

2. _____ When you read a poem, you probably need to know math.

3. _____ When you are deciding how much paint to buy to paint your bedroom, you are using math.

Challenge Words

Check (✔) the words you already know.

☐ algebra   ☐ arithmetic   ☐ geometry   ☐ trigonometry

46. Choice

Check (✔) the words you already know. Then, listen and repeat.

Tracks 1–8

☐ **judge**
TR 1

☐ **appoint**
TR 2

Definitions

To **appoint** someone to a job or a position means to choose that person for it.

Your **choice** is the thing or things that you choose.

To **choose** someone or something means to decide to have that specific person or thing.

If you **decide** to do something, you choose to do it after thinking about it.

If you **judge** a competition, you decide who is the winner.

To **pick** a particular person or thing means to choose that specific one.

To **select** means to choose something from a group of similar things.

To **sort** means to separate items into different groups.

☐ **sort**
TR 3

☐ **choice**
TR 4

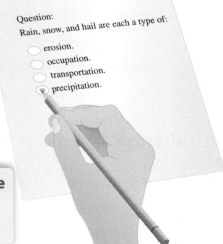

Question:
Rain, snow, and hail are each a type of:
○ erosion.
○ occupation.
○ transportation.
● precipitation.

☐ **decide**
TR 5

☐ **choose**
☐ **pick**
☐ **select**
TR 6, 7, and 8

Check Your Understanding

A. Underline the correct word to complete each sentence.

1. Let's (**choose** / **sort**) these papers into piles to organize them.

2. It is so difficult to (**choose** / **appoint**) a color when they all look so pretty.

3. Your meal at the restaurant was so much better than mine. I made the wrong (**appoint** / **choice**).

4. Who has been (**sorted** / **appointed**) as the new head of the Police Department?

5. Laura was (**sorted** / **picked**) for the lead role in this year's school play.

6. After thinking about it, Michael (**judged** / **decided**) to save his work on the computer.

7. The people who (**judge** / **appoint**) the baking contest must taste each dessert.

8. Which book did Nora (**judge** / **select**) for her book report?

B. Choose the sentence that correctly uses the underlined word.

1. a. It was my <u>choice</u> to go to this restaurant.

   b. Let's go to the <u>choice</u> for dinner.

2. a. Anna <u>chooses</u> with Maria after school every day.

   b. Anna <u>chooses</u> to do her homework in the library, not at home.

3. a. What movie did you <u>decide</u> to see?

   b. When do you <u>decide</u> breakfast each morning?

4. a. Amy will <u>judge</u> the blue shirt.

   b. Amy will <u>judge</u> the talent show.

5. a. John <u>picked</u> Robert to play on his team in the baseball game.

   b. It started to rain so Robert <u>picked</u> home.

6. a. How many items can we <u>select</u> from the list?

   b. We <u>select</u> in the park on our bicycles.

7. a. The coach <u>appointed</u> the team in the competition.

   b. They <u>appointed</u> the coach to the job of Athletic Director.

8. a. The photos were <u>sorted</u> by date.

   b. The photos showed the people <u>sorting</u> on the beach.

Challenge Words

Check (✔) the words you already know.

- [ ] assign
- [ ] decision
- [ ] dedicate
- [ ] discriminate
- [ ] judgment
- [ ] verdict
- [ ] weed

67. Memory / Thought (General)

Check (✔) the words you already know. Then, listen and repeat.

 Tracks 1–8

☐ **forget**
TR 1

☐ **idea**
☐ **thought**
TR 2 and TR 3

☐ **imagine**
TR 4

Definitions

If you **forget** something, you do not remember it.

An **idea** is a thought, especially a new one.

If you **imagine** something, you form a picture or idea of it in your mind.

A **memory** is something that you remember from the past.

If you **remember** people or events from the past, you still have an idea of them in your mind.

When you **think**, you use your mind to consider something.

A **thought** is an idea or an opinion.

If you **wonder** about something, you think about it and try to guess or understand more about it.

☐ **memory**
TR 5

☐ **think**
TR 6

☐ **wonder**
TR 7

☐ **remember**
TR 8

Check Your Understanding

A. Match each word to the correct description. One description will not be used.

1. _____ forget
2. _____ idea
3. _____ remember
4. _____ think
5. _____ thought
6. _____ wonder
7. _____ imagine
8. _____ memory

a. when you try to guess or understand something
b. what you have in your mind when you think
c. the word for a new thought
d. a thought about the past
e. what you do when asleep
f. the opposite of *forget*
g. what you do when you have a thought
h. the opposite of *remember*
i. what you do when you picture something in your mind

B. Read the dialogue between Eddy and Jon. Underline the correct word to complete each sentence.

Eddy: Hi Jon. Did you (1) (**forget / imagine**) that we have a Math test today?

Jon: I was sure that we had an English test, but not Math. I (2) (**wonder / think**) what is going to be on it.

Eddy: I (3) (**wonder / think**) it will cover what we learned in the last two lessons.

Jon: Oh, no! That was so hard. I had no (4) (**idea / memory**) we would have a test so soon!

Eddy: Just relax while you are taking the test. (5) (**Imagine / Forget**) that you will get a perfect grade.

Jon: It's easy for you to have (6) (**thoughts / memories**) about getting a great grade. You are good at Math!

Eddy: Don't worry! By tomorrow this Math test will only be a (7) (**thought / memory**).

Challenge Words

Check (✔) the words you already know.

☐ concentrate   ☐ consider   ☐ imagination   ☐ recall
☐ concept   ☐ contemplate   ☐ memorize   ☐ visualize

132. Consciousness / Unconsciousness

Check (✔) the words you already know. Then, listen and repeat.

 Tracks 1–8

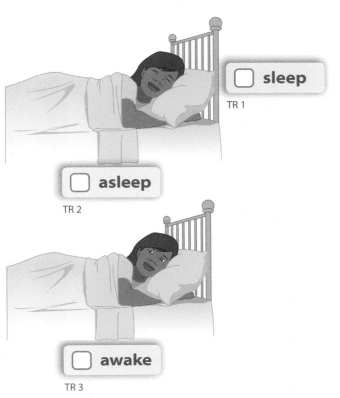

- [ ] sleep
TR 1

- [ ] asleep
TR 2

- [ ] awake
TR 3

Definitions

Someone who is **asleep** is sleeping.

Someone who is **awake** is not sleeping.

When you **daydream**, you think about pleasant things while you are awake.

When you **dream**, you see events in your mind while you are asleep.

A **nap** is a short sleep that you have, usually during the day.

To **pretend** means to make believe that a situation is true, even when it is not.

To **sleep** means to rest your body and your mind. You close your eyes when you **sleep**.

To **wake** means to stop sleeping.

- [ ] dream
TR 4

- [ ] nap
TR 5

- [ ] daydream
TR 8

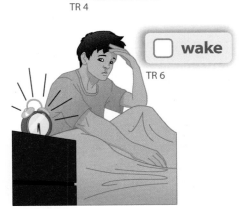

- [ ] wake
TR 6

- [ ] pretend
TR 7

Check Your Understanding

A. Circle the correct word to complete each sentence.

1. Charles was _____ when the phone rang, so he missed the call.

   a. pretending   b. asleep   c. awake

2. I usually _____ at 7 A.M. every morning.

   a. dream   b. daydream   c. wake

3. The teacher complained that Suzette was always _____ in class and didn't pay attention.

   a. daydreaming   b. awake   c. waking

4. Maria was so tired after school that she went right home for a _____.

   a. daydream   b. dream   c. nap

5. How many hours should people _____ each night?

   a. sleep   b. wake   c. pretend

6. My little cousin likes to _____ that he is a superhero.

   a. pretend   b. wake   c. sleep

7. Andrea told us about the funny things she _____ last night.

   a. slept   b. woke   c. dreamed

8. When she heard the baby crying, she knew he was _____.

   a. asleep   b. awake   c. napping

B. Choose the correct word from the word bank to complete each sentence.

nap	dreamed	sleep	wake
asleep	pretended	awake	daydreams

1. My father had to _____ me this morning because I did not hear my alarm.
2. While she was playing, Meg _____ that her toy bear could talk.
3. At night, I _____ in the bedroom on the third floor.
4. I _____ that I was in London, but when I woke up I was at home.
5. I may not be able to stay _____ for the late movie because I am tired.
6. Sandra often _____ about finding a better job while she is at work.
7. Lena was very tired. She was _____ by 7:00 P.M.
8. My grandfather takes a 20-minute _____ every afternoon at two o'clock.

Challenge Words

Check (✔) the words you already know.

- [ ] conscious
- [ ] drowsy
- [ ] hibernate
- [ ] snooze
- [ ] doze
- [ ] fantasy
- [ ] nightmare
- [ ] weary

137. Intelligence

Check (✔) the words you already know. Then, listen and repeat.

Tracks 1–6

☐ **able**

TR 1

☐ **alert**

TR 4

☐ **smart**

TR 2

☐ **stupid**

TR 3

Definitions

When you are **able** to do something, you have the skills or qualities that make it possible for you to do it.

When you are **alert**, you are paying attention and are ready to deal with anything that might happen.

A **brilliant** person, idea, or performance is very clever or skillful.

A **smart** person is someone who is very clever or intelligent.

When someone or something seems or acts **stupid**, they behave in a way that is foolish or unintelligent.

A **wise** person shares and uses their experience and knowledge to make good decisions and judgments.

☐ **wise**

TR 6

☐ **brilliant**

TR 5

Einstein was **brilliant**.

Check Your Understanding

A. Choose the correct word from the box to complete each sentence.

able	alert	wise
smart	stupid	brilliant

1. Andrew is a _____ painter. His work is the best that I've seen.

2. How is Wendy _____ to write with a broken arm?

3. It would be _____ to pull the fire alarm at the school if there wasn't a fire.

4. Christine needs to be _____ at work. Otherwise, she will make a mistake.

5. Ana is very _____. She can always answer the teacher's questions and gets good grades.

6. People go to Mr. Sanders for business advice. He is very _____ after 30 years with the company.

B. Match each word to the correct example. One example will not be used.

1. _____ able
2. _____ smart
3. _____ stupid
4. _____ alert
5. _____ brilliant
6. _____ wise

a. a police offer who is on duty at night

b. a man asking another person what time it is

c. a mother giving advice to her children about life

d. a four-year-old who can read books without an adult's help

e. a clever, unique idea that will help you solve a problem

f. a person who has the right experience for a job

g. a teenager who drives her parents' car without permission

Challenge Words

Check (✔) the words you already know.

☐ aware   ☐ clever   ☐ curious   ☐ intelligent

☐ capable   ☐ creative   ☐ ignorant   ☐ wisdom

154. Learning and Teaching

Check (✔) the words you already know. Then, listen and repeat.

Tracks 1–16

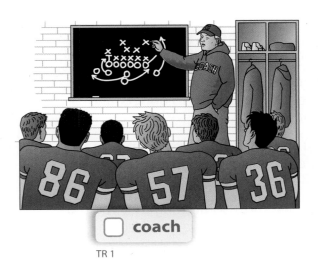

☐ **coach**

TR 1

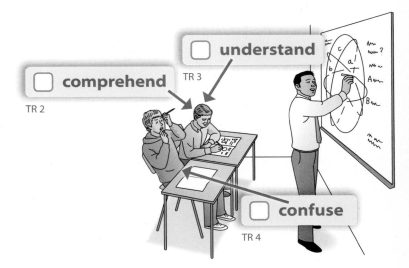

☐ **comprehend**

TR 2

☐ **understand**

TR 3

☐ **confuse**

TR 4

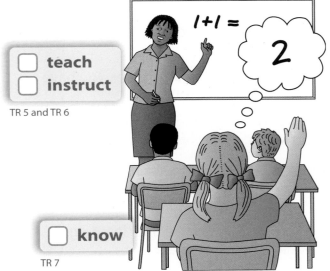

☐ **teach**
☐ **instruct**

TR 5 and TR 6

☐ **know**

TR 7

☐ **learn**

TR 8

college

☐ **direction**

TR 9

☐ **advice**

TR 10

I did not know that Hong Kong is an island.

☐ **discover**
TR 11

☐ **study**
TR 12

☐ **suggest**
TR 13

☐ **trick**
TR 14

INFORMATION

☐ **information**
TR 15

☐ **outsmart**
TR 16

Definitions

If you give someone **advice**, you give a suggestion or your opinion about something.

If you **coach** someone, you help that person become better at a particular sport or skill.

If you **comprehend** something, you understand it.

To **confuse** someone means to make it hard for that person to understand something.

If you give someone **direction**, you provide leadership or guidance to help people reach certain goals.

If you **discover** something that you did not know about before, you become aware of it.

Information about someone or something is facts about that person or thing.

If you **instruct** someone in a subject, you teach it to a person.

If you **know** a fact or an answer, you have that information in your mind.

If you **learn** something, you gain knowledge about it.

If you **outsmart** someone, you find a clever way to be better or more successful than someone else.

If you **study**, you spend time learning about a particular subject.

If you **suggest** something, you tell someone what you think that person should do.

If you **teach** someone, you give instructions about a topic or a subject.

A **trick** is a clever action that someone or something does to entertain or confuse others.

If you **understand** something, you know what it means, or why or how it happens.

Check Your Understanding

A. Circle the correct answer to complete each sentence.

1. If someone is *coaching* you, she is _____ .
   a. helping you play a sport
   b. building a house for you
   c. reminding you to eat

2. When you ask for *direction,* you want to know _____ .
   a. why something is the way it is
   b. how to do something
   c. how to trick someone

3. When you *know* something, you _____ .
   a. like it
   b. do not like it
   c. have information about it

4. When you *learn* something, you _____ .
   a. cannot say anything about it
   b. can explain it to someone else
   c. are unable to do it

5. When somebody *teaches,* she _____ .
   a. cooks very well
   b. helps you to learn something
   c. does a lot of exercise

6. When you *understand* something, _____ .
   a. it makes sense to you
   b. it is unclear to you
   c. you don't know about it

7. If you give a person *advice,* you _____ .
   a. hurt his feelings
   b. fool him into doing something
   c. give an opinion about what he should do

8. When you *comprehend* something, you _____ .
   a. teach it
   b. understand it
   c. want it

9. When a person *confuses* another person, he is _____ .
   a. being helpful
   b. teaching the person
   c. making it hard for the person to understand him

10. You *discover* something when _____ .
    a. you become aware of it
    b. you pay for it
    c. you teach others about it

11. You might ask for *information* if you want to _____ .
    a. visit a new place
    b. confuse someone
    c. give directions to a place

12. Another word for *instruct* is _____ .
    a. teach
    b. confuse
    c. understand

13. When you *outsmart* somebody, you _____ .
    a. help her to learn something
    b. solve a problem faster than her
    c. understand her

14. When you *study,* you _____ .
    a. prepare for a test
    b. teach someone something
    c. explain how to play a sport

15. When a friend *suggests* something, he _____.

   a. thinks it is a good idea   b. doesn't want you to do it   c. is trying to confuse you

16. When you do a *trick*, you try to _____.

   a. teach someone   b. entertain someone   c. coach someone

B. Underline the correct word to complete each sentence.

1. For his last (**trick / discover**), the magician pulled a rabbit out of his hat.

2. Who will (**confuse / coach**) the All-Star Team this year?

3. What subject does your aunt (**suggest / teach**) at the high school?

4. My guidance counselor's (**direction / information**) made me realize that I wanted to be a doctor.

5. Anne (**instructed / outsmarted**) the students on how to solve the difficult math problem.

6. The player (**taught / outsmarted**) his opponent and got control of the ball.

7. Andy (**studied / tricked**) for hours, but he did poorly on his history test.

8. Our teacher (**comprehended / suggested**) that we read the chapters in order.

9. My little brother does not (**know / teach**) how to tie his shoes yet, but he tries.

10. Tony is (**learning / confusing**) Spanish in school, and he is starting to speak it well.

11. I cannot (**comprehend / suggest**) why you do those crossword puzzles when you find them so difficult.

12. Today is Tuesday? I was (**discovered / confused**) and thought it was Monday.

13. Do you have any (**advice / tricks**) for me? I want to exercise more, but I don't know which kind is best.

14. Greta just (**discovered / understood**) twenty dollars in the pocket of her coat.

15. I would like to visit Japan, but I do not (**coach / understand**) Japanese.

16. Where can I get more (**information / advice**) about Chicago? I would like to visit there.

Challenge Words

Check (✔) the words you already know.

☐ breakthrough   ☐ educate   ☐ input   ☐ realize

☐ complicate   ☐ fake   ☐ mystify   ☐ suggestion

225. Mental Exploration

Check (✔) the words you already know. Then, listen and repeat.

Tracks 1–10

☐ **explore**

TR 1

☐ **homework**

TR 2

☐ **analyze**

TR 3

☐ **news**

TR 4

☐ **search**

TR 6

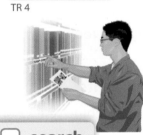

☐ **examine**

TR 5

☐ **lesson**

TR 7

☐ **schoolwork**

TR 8

☐ **experiment**

TR 9

☐ **investigate**

TR 10

Definitions

If you **analyze** something, you consider it carefully in order to fully understand it.

If you **examine** someone or something, you look at a person or it carefully.

An **experiment** is a scientific test you do in order to discover what happens.

If you **explore** a place, you travel around it to find out what it is like.

Homework is schoolwork that teachers give to students to do outside of class time.

If you **investigate** something, you try to find out what happened.

A **lesson** is a time when you learn about a particular subject.

News is information about recent events that is reported in newspapers, or on the radio, television, or Internet.

Schoolwork is the work that a student does at school or work that teachers give students to do at home.

If you **search** for someone or something, you look for a person or for it carefully.

Check Your Understanding

A. Circle the correct word to complete each sentence.

1. Were you in music class yesterday for the _____ about rap?
   a. search   b. news   c. lesson

2. The police are _____ to find the cause of the accident.
   a. exploring   b. experimenting   c. investigating

3. Is there _____ for math class tonight? If not, I will leave my textbook at school.
   a. homework   b. news   c. lesson

4. Callie _____ for an hour for her car keys but could not find them.
   a. examined   b. searched   c. explored

5. Did you see on the _____ that Main Street is closed due to flooding?
   a. experiment   b. news   c. lesson

6. Be sure to _____ the text carefully so that you will understand it well.
   a. explore   b. search   c. analyze

7. The doctor _____ the girl's hand, but it wasn't broken.
   a. investigated   b. examined   c. explored

8. I'm looking forward to chemistry class today so I can record the results of my lab _____.
   a. experiment   b. examine   c. lesson

9. Now that we are in the tenth grade, our _____ is much more difficult.
   a. news   b. experiment   c. schoolwork

10. They spent the weekend _____ New York City and found new, fun places to visit.
    a. analyzing   b. exploring   c. experimenting

B. Write **T** for **true statements** and **F** for **false statements**.

1. _____ You can find out what is in the news by watching television.

2. _____ If you lose something, you will probably search for it.

3. _____ When you analyze something, you make a quick decision.

4. _____ A dentist may examine the inside of your mouth.

5. _____ During an experiment, you find out what will happen.

6. _____ You can explore by looking out the window.

7. _____ You might do your homework in your bedroom.

8. _____ When you investigate something, you ask a lot of questions about it.

9. _____ Lessons after school are the only way to learn dance or music.

10. _____ Most students do not have schoolwork.

Challenge Words

Check (✔) the words you already know.

☐ hypothesis   ☐ inspect   ☐ probe   ☐ review

☐ imprint   ☐ inspection   ☐ research   ☐ survey

20

249. Conclusions

Check (✔) the words you already know. Then, listen and repeat.

Tracks 1–17

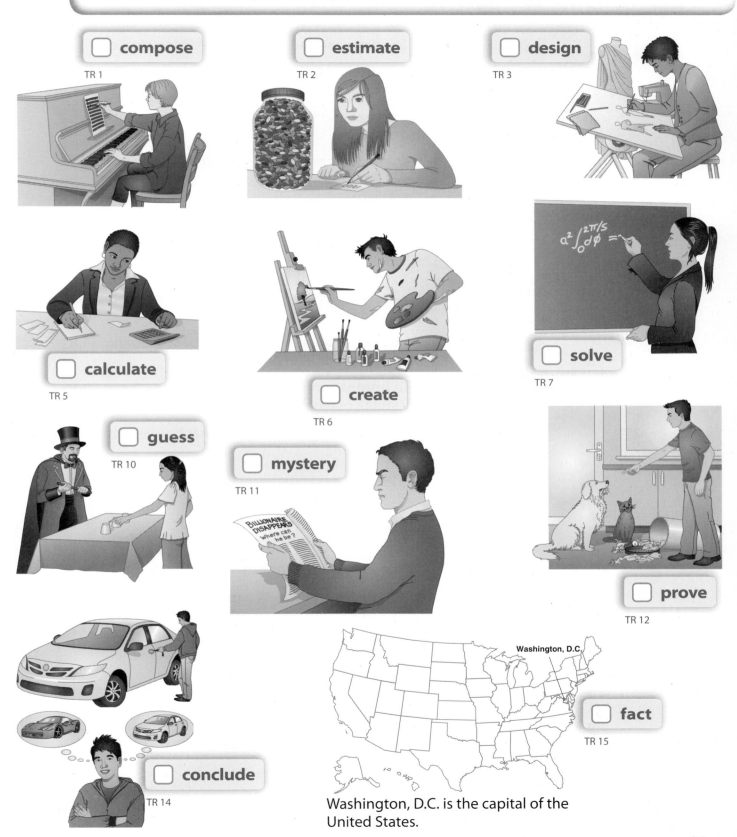

☐ **compose**
TR 1

☐ **estimate**
TR 2

☐ **design**
TR 3

☐ **calculate**
TR 5

☐ **create**
TR 6

☐ **solve**
TR 7

☐ **guess**
TR 10

☐ **mystery**
TR 11

☐ **prove**
TR 12

☐ **conclude**
TR 14

Washington, D.C.

☐ **fact**
TR 15

Washington, D.C. is the capital of the United States.

"Do you **suppose** the home team will win?"

☐ **suppose**

TR 4

☐ **invention**

TR 8

☐ **invent**

TR 9

☐ **clue**

TR 13

☐ **information**

TR 16

INFORMATION

Definitions

To **calculate** an amount means to find it out by using numbers.

A **clue** is information that helps you to find an answer to a question.

To **compose** music or text means to create it.

To **conclude** means to make a decision after thinking about something carefully.

To **create** something means to make it happen or exist.

To **design** something new means to plan what it will be like.

To **estimate** the amount or value of something means to say how much you think there is of it.

A **fact** is information that is true.

To **guess** means to give an answer or an opinion when you do not know if your answer or opinion is true.

Information about someone or something is facts about that person or place.

To **invent** something means to be the first person to think of it or make it.

An **invention** is something that has been invented by someone.

A **mystery** is something that you cannot explain or understand.

To **predict** an event means to guess that it will happen in the future.

To **prove** means to show that something is true.

To **solve** a problem or a question means to find an answer to it.

To **suppose** means to imagine that something could be true.

☐ **predict**

TR 17

Check Your Understanding

A. Circle the correct definition for each word.

1. guess
   a. to tell another person what to do
   b. to say what you think might happen

2. calculate
   a. to find the total number of something
   b. to find out facts about something

3. clue
   a. information that helps you answer a question
   b. an answer to a question

4. compose
   a. to play a piece of music or read a text
   b. to create a piece of music or a text

5. conclude
   a. to decide
   b. to discover

6. create
   a. to make
   b. to learn

7. design
   a. to save money for a special gift
   b. to plan something before it is created

8. estimate
   a. to calculate the total number of something
   b. to carefully guess at the total number of something

9. fact
   a. something that is true
   b. something that may be true

10. information
    a. problems that you have with something
    b. facts that you have about something

11. invent
    a. to create something new
    b. to look for information on how to do something

12. invention
    a. a new object or idea that somebody has just created
    b. an idea about what will happen in the future

13. mystery
    a. something that you can easily solve
    b. something that you cannot understand

14. predict
    a. to say what you think happened in the past
    b. to say what you think will happen in the future

15. prove
    a. to show that something is true
    b. to hope that something is true

16. solve
    a. to find a way to fix a problem
    b. to guess at the answer to a question

17. suppose
    a. to imagine that something is true
    b. to show that something is true

B. Circle the correct word to complete each sentence.

1. I _____ that we will have homework tomorrow night, since we don't have any tonight.
   - a. invent
   - b. prove
   - c. suppose

2. Paula sat at the desk to _____ the letter.
   - a. guess
   - b. compose
   - c. solve

3. Can you _____ where we are going tomorrow?
   - a. create
   - b. compose
   - c. guess

4. Janie tried to _____ the difficult math problem, but she could not.
   - a. solve
   - b. estimate
   - c. invent

5. Leslie went skydiving to _____ that she was not afraid to do it.
   - a. suppose
   - b. prove
   - c. estimate

6. The weatherman is _____ rain for the entire weekend.
   - a. designing
   - b. composing
   - c. predicting

7. Tom _____ that it was easier to walk to school than to ride his bicycle.
   - a. composed
   - b. concluded
   - c. created

8. It is a _____ to me why I keep losing one sock out of a pair.
   - a. fact
   - b. clue
   - c. mystery

9. This new _____ tells me how many steps I have walked today.
   - a. clue
   - b. invention
   - c. fact

10. The architect _____ the house so that all the rooms are on one floor.
    - a. designed
    - b. supposed
    - c. estimated

11. Lily _____ flower pots from recycled plastic.
    - a. estimated
    - b. guessed
    - c. created

12. Event organizers _____ that 2,000 people will attend Saturday's concert.
    - a. compose
    - b. prove
    - c. estimate

13. Henry has _____ that it will take him three weeks to do the project.
    - a. invented
    - b. calculated
    - c. solved

14. The police are still looking for _____ to help them to find the car thief.
    - a. mysteries
    - b. clues
    - c. inventions

15. When did Thomas Edison _____ the lightbulb?
    - a. invent
    - b. compose
    - c. conclude

16. Natalie asked the doctor for _____ on how to eat properly.
    - a. inventions
    - b. mysteries
    - c. information

17. Health officials have published a booklet with _____ about the dangers of driving while text messaging.
    - a. facts
    - b. mysteries
    - c. clues

Challenge Words

Check (✔) the words you already know.

- ☐ assume
- ☐ determine
- ☐ evaluate
- ☐ forecast
- ☐ confirm
- ☐ discovery
- ☐ evidence
- ☐ prediction

277. Topics and Subjects

Check (✔) the words you already know. Then, listen and repeat.

Tracks 1–4

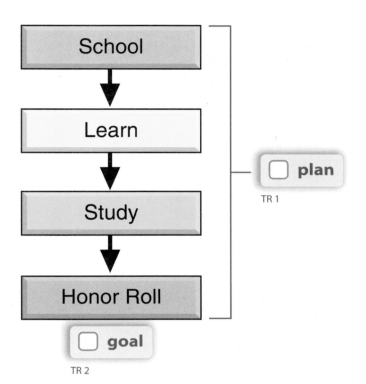

School

↓

Learn

↓

Study

↓

Honor Roll

☐ **plan**
TR 1

☐ **goal**
TR 2

Definitions

Your **goal** is the aim or purpose that you have when you do something.

A **plan** is a series of steps that you think about in advance in order to help you reach a goal.

A **subject** is an area of knowledge that you study in school or college.

A **topic** is a particular subject that you talk or write about.

English Essay:

Youth Rebellion in
The Catcher in the Rye

☐ **topic**
TR 4

☐ **subject**
TR 3

Check Your Understanding

A. Complete the story with the correct words from the word bank.

goal	plan	subject	topics

My favorite (1) _____ in school is drama. I love to read plays and talk about the interesting (2) _____ with my teacher and my classmates.

I would like to become an actor. My (3) _____ is to get a part in this year's school play. I need to prepare for the audition, though. My (4) _____ is to work with my teacher and practice by myself at home each night for three weeks before the audition. If I work hard, I know I will get a good part!

B. Match each word to the correct example. One example will not be used.

1. _____ goal
2. _____ plan
3. _____ subject
4. _____ topic

a. a way of looking at something
b. how to fix cars
c. Language Arts
d. to go to the gym regularly and eat healthy foods
e. to lose ten pounds in three months

Challenge Words

Check (✔) the words you already know.

☐ essence   ☐ scheme   ☐ strategy   ☐ thesis
☐ objective   ☐ scope   ☐ theme   ☐ viewpoint

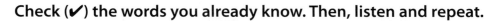

347. Interest

Check (✔) the words you already know. Then, listen and repeat.

Tracks 1–2

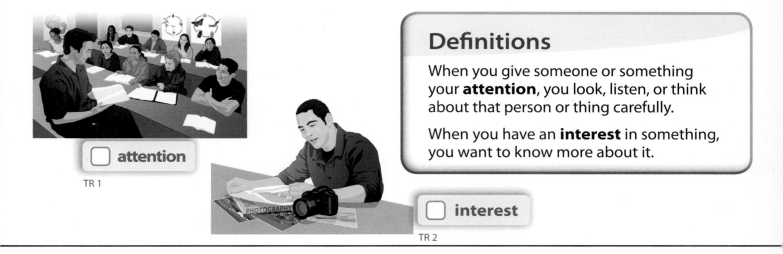

☐ **attention**

TR 1

Definitions

When you give someone or something your **attention**, you look, listen, or think about that person or thing carefully.

When you have an **interest** in something, you want to know more about it.

☐ **interest**

TR 2

Check Your Understanding

A. Choose the correct word from the word bank to complete each sentence. One word will be used twice.

attention	interest

1. Lynn has no _____ in learning how to cook. She would much rather go out to a restaurant.

2. Michael's teacher told his parents that he always pays _____ in class.

3. Gina could not tell her friends about the show because she did not give it her full _____ while it was on.

B. Write **T** for **true statements** and **F** for **false statements**.

1. _____ If you have an interest in something, you try to stay away from it.

2. _____ If you are listening to what somebody is telling you, you are paying attention that person.

3. _____ An actor probably has an interest in movies and television.

4. _____ Your teacher does not want you to pay attention in class.

Challenge Words

Check (✔) the words you already know.

☐ concentration   ☐ curiosity   ☐ intrigue

348. Procedures and Processes

Check (✔) the words you already know. Then, listen and repeat.

Tracks 1–3

☐ **routine**

TR 1

☐ **process**

TR 2

Check Your Understanding

A. Choose the correct word from the word bank to complete each sentence.

process	recipe	routine

1. The _____ says that I need three eggs and a teaspoon of salt.

2. Can you describe the _____ of getting a passport?

3. Stopping by the coffee shop was part of Jim's morning _____ .

recipe

TR 3

Definitions

A **process** is a series of actions that have a particular result.

A **recipe** is a list of food and a set of instructions telling you how to cook something.

A **routine** is a series of usual activities that a person does every day or very often.

B. Underline the correct word to complete each sentence.

1. Allison broke from her (**recipe / routine**) when she slept in until ten o'clock yesterday.

2. This cheese is for my (**recipe / process**) for cheese soup.

3. Applying for college is a very long and difficult (**routine / process**).

Challenge Words

Check (✔) the words you already know.

☐ function   ☐ method   ☐ system

☐ logic   ☐ procedure   ☐ technique

349. Beliefs

Check (✔) the words you already know. Then, listen and repeat.

Tracks 1–2

I will win this race.

Quiz

1. Circle the statement that is an opinion.

A: Madrid is the capital of Spain.

B: Spain is the best country to visit in Europe.

Definitions

A **belief** is a powerful feeling that something is real or true.

Your **opinion** of something is what you think about it.

☐ **belief**

TR 1

☐ **opinion**

TR 2

Check Your Understanding

A. Complete each sentence using either *belief* or *opinion*.

1. What you think of a person or thing is your _____.

2. When you really think that something is true, it is a _____.

3. Juana said it was only her _____, but she doesn't think spaghetti tastes good.

B. Write **T** for **true statements** and **F** for **false statements**.

1. _____ Everybody has the same opinions about television shows.

2. _____ A belief is a strong feeling that something is true.

3. _____ Your best friend might have different opinions than you do.

4. _____ *Belief* means the same as *opinion*.

Challenge Words

Check (✔) the words you already know.

☐ custom   ☐ ideal   ☐ mythology   ☐ superstition

☐ habit   ☐ instinct   ☐ philosophy   ☐ tradition

384. Definition / Meaning

Check (✔) the word if you already know it. Then, listen and repeat.

Track 1

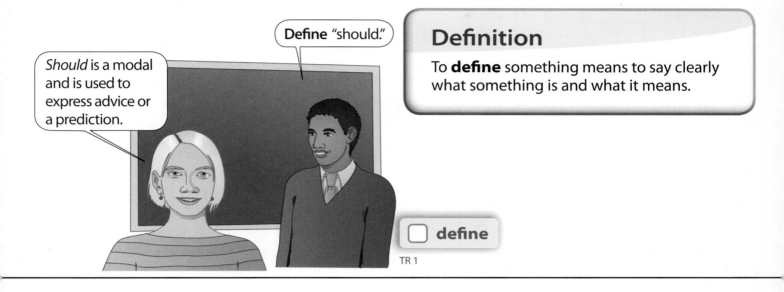

Should is a modal and is used to express advice or a prediction.

Define "should."

Definition

To **define** something means to say clearly what something is and what it means.

☐ define

TR 1

Check Your Understanding

A. Write **T** for **true statements** and **F** for **false statements**.

1. _____ When you define something, you say what it means.

2. _____ If you cannot define a word, you should look in the dictionary.

3. _____ If you define something, you do not know what it means.

B. Choose the sentence that correctly uses the underlined word.

1. a. Valerie had to <u>define</u> ten words for homework.

   b. Valerie had to <u>define</u> ten questions for homework last night.

2. a. I <u>define</u> to the library on Tuesday.

   b. How do you <u>define</u> "happy"?

3. a. Joseph was able to <u>define</u> the chemistry terms for Dave.

   b. Joseph could not <u>define</u> the high jump in gym class.

Challenge Words

Check (✔) the words you already know.

☐ definition   ☐ interpret   ☐ meaning   ☐ represent

172. Locations Where People Might Live

Check (✔) the words you already know. Then, listen and repeat.

Tracks 1–12

☐ **city**

TR 1

☐ **neighborhood**

TR 2

☐ **town**

TR 3

☐ **downtown**

TR 5

☐ **suburb**

TR 6

☐ **village**

TR 7

☐ **camp**

TR 9

☐ **ghetto**

TR 10

Check Your Understanding

A. Underline the correct word to complete each sentence.

1. Larry lives out in the (**suburbs / slums**), in a house with a large yard.

2. Miami is one of my favorite (**cities / camps**) to visit.

3. This home is on a quiet street in a nice (**heaven / neighborhood**).

4. After they finish skiing, Rosa and Paul like to go into the nearby (**village / slum**) to eat dinner.

5. There is a (**state / camp**) right near the lake. Let's bring our tents and spend the weekend there.

6. My aunt lives in San Diego, in the (**state / county**) of California.

7. On the main street of our (**town / state**), you will find a drugstore and a post office.

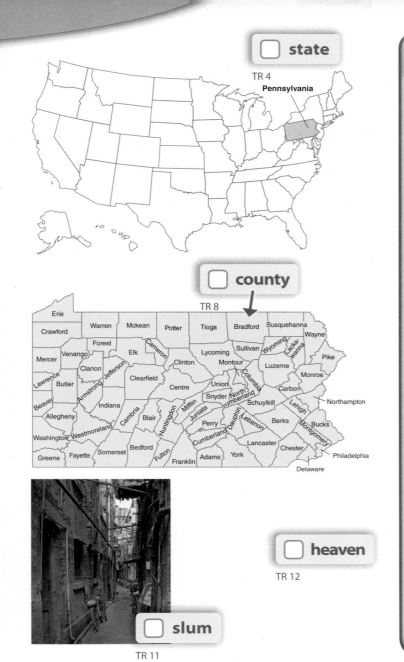

state

TR 4

Pennsylvania

county

TR 8

Erie, Crawford, Warren, Mckean, Potter, Tioga, Bradford, Susquehanna, Wayne, Forest, Cameron, Lycoming, Sullivan, Wyoming, Lacka-wanna, Pike, Mercer, Venango, Elk, Clinton, Montour, Luzerne, Monroe, Lawrence, Clarion, Jefferson, Clearfield, Centre, Columbia, Carbon, Butler, Armstrong, Union, Snyder, North-umberland, Schuylkill, Lehigh, Northampton, Beaver, Indiana, Cambria, Mifflin, Juniata, Dauphin, Lebanon, Berks, Bucks, Allegheny, Blair, Huntingdon, Perry, Montgomery, Washington, Westmoreland, Cumberland, Lancaster, Chester, Philadelphia, Greene, Fayette, Somerset, Bedford, Fulton, Franklin, Adams, York, Delaware

heaven

TR 12

slum

TR 11

Definitions

A **camp** is a place outdoors where people stay in tents, usually for a short period of time.

A **city** is an area with many people living and working close together.

A **county** is a small area of a state or country that usually includes several cities.

Downtown is the business center part of a city.

A **ghetto** is usually a poor area of a city.

Heaven is a place where some people believe good people go to when they die.

A **neighborhood** is one of the parts of a town where people live.

A **slum** is a poor area of a city where the buildings are in bad condition and the living conditions are poor.

A **state** is a place that has its own government and laws in addition to those of the country.

A **suburb** is a small city or town, usually outside of a big city, where people live. A **suburb** usually has more houses than businesses.

A **town** is a place with many streets, buildings, and stores, where people live and work. A **town** is smaller than a city.

A **village** is a small town in the countryside.

8. The mayor promised to improve the (**heaven / ghetto**) by bringing more jobs to the area.

9. What time does this train arrive (**downtown / neighborhood**)? I have a meeting at the Central Bank at ten o'clock.

10. My friend believes that all good pets go to (**heaven / suburbs**) when they die.

11. That building was in very poor condition and many people complained that it was a (**slum / suburb**).

12. Every (**county / camp**) in the state has a fair in the summer, and people come from towns in the area to have fun.

B. Match each word to the correct description. One description will not be used.

1. _____ city
2. _____ neighborhood
3. _____ state
4. _____ town
5. _____ village
6. _____ camp
7. _____ county
8. _____ downtown
9. _____ ghetto
10. _____ heaven
11. _____ slum
12. _____ suburb

a. a very small town that is found in the country
b. a place with its own government that is part of a country
c. the center part of a city
d. an area with many people and buildings
e. a place where people go to sleep outside
f. smaller area within a state
g. a part of a large city where the buildings are in bad condition
h. a place where, some people believe, good people go after death
i. a place where people live and work that is smaller than a city
j. the place where you were born
k. the part of town where you and your neighbors live
l. a poor area of a city
m. a place where people live outside of a city

Challenge Words

Check (✔) the words you already know.

- ☐ birthplace
- ☐ capital
- ☐ colony
- ☐ district
- ☐ empire
- ☐ homeland
- ☐ kingdom
- ☐ outskirts

180. Countries and Continents

Check (✔) the words you already know. Then, listen and repeat.

Tracks 1–5

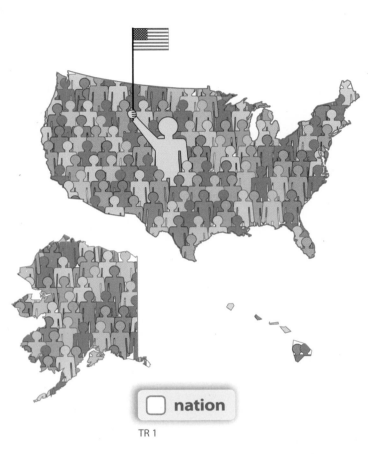

Definitions

A **continent** is a very large area of land, such as North America or Asia.

A **country** is an area of the world with its own government and people.

The **equator** is an imaginary line around the middle of the Earth.

A **hemisphere** is one half of the Earth.

A **nation** is an individual country, its people, and its social and political structures.

☐ **nation**

TR 1

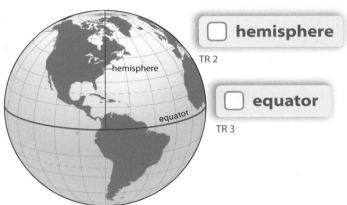

hemisphere

equator

☐ **hemisphere**

TR 2

☐ **equator**

TR 3

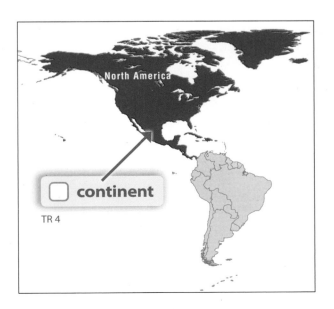

North America

☐ **continent**

TR 4

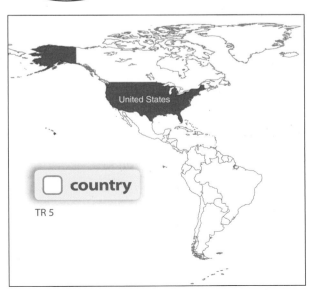

United States

☐ **country**

TR 5

Check Your Understanding

A. Write **T** for **true statements** and **F** for **false statements**.

1. _____ A country does not have a government.

2. _____ The equator is a line that shows a country's border.

3. _____ A hemisphere is one half of the Earth.

4. _____ A nation is an individual country and its people.

5. _____ A continent is a small area of land.

B. Underline the correct word to complete each sentence.

1. Asia and North America are examples of (**continents / equators**).

2. The people who live in this (**equator / country**) follow the rule of their government.

3. The imaginary line around the middle of the Earth is the (**equator / nation**).

4. Half of the Earth is called a (**hemisphere / continent**).

5. Algeria is an individual country, or (**hemisphere / nation**), that is located in Africa.

Challenge Words

Check (✔) the words you already know.

☐ nationwide   ☐ sovereign

43. Sadness

Check (✔) the words you already know. Then, listen and repeat.

Tracks 1–3

☐ **sad**

TR 1

Definitions

When you are **sad**, you feel unhappy.

When you are **sorry** about a situation, you feel regret, sadness, or disappointment about it.

When you are **unhappy** about something, you are not satisfied with it.

I'm **sorry** that I forgot your birthday.

☐ **sorry**

TR 3

☐ **unhappy**

TR 2

Check Your Understanding

A. Choose the correct word from the word bank to complete each sentence.

sad	sorry	unhappy

1. Miguel said he was _____ because he regretted missing his sister's piano recital.

2. Why are you so _____? You have been crying all day.

3. My parents will be _____ if I do not clean my room.

B. Choose the sentence that correctly uses the underlined word.

1. a. After she saw the A+ on her report card, Claire was very <u>unhappy</u>.

   b. After she saw the F on her report card, Claire was very <u>unhappy</u>.

2. a. The entire family was <u>sad</u> when they brought a new cat home.

   b. The entire family was <u>sad</u> when their cat died.

3. a. Maggie was <u>sorry</u> that she lost her mother's car keys.

   a. Maggie was <u>sorry</u> that her mother let her borrow the new car.

Challenge Words

Check (✔) the words you already know.

- ☐ dismay
- ☐ grief
- ☐ loneliness
- ☐ sorrow
- ☐ gloom
- ☐ heartache
- ☐ misery
- ☐ suffer

45. Fun and Joy

Check (✔) the words you already know. Then, listen and repeat.

Tracks 1–14

☐ **please**
TR 1

☐ **silly**
TR 2

☐ **happiness**
☐ **joy**
TR 3 and TR 4

☐ **glad**
☐ **happy**
TR 5 and TR 6

☐ **humor**
TR 7

☐ **play**
TR 8

☐ **joke**
TR 9

Definitions

To **celebrate** means to do something enjoyable for a special reason.

Fun is pleasure and enjoyment.

When you are **glad** about something, you are happy and pleased about it.

Happiness is a feeling of joy or contentment.

Someone who is **happy** feels pleased and satisfied.

Humor is the quality of being funny.

A **joke** is something that someone says or does to make you laugh.

Someone who is **jolly** is happy and cheerful.

Joy is a feeling of great happiness.

Something that is **joyful** causes happiness and pleasure.

Merry means happy and cheerful.

When people or animals **play**, they spend time using toys and taking part in games.

To **please** means to make someone or something feel happy and satisfied.

When you are **silly**, you do not behave in a sensible or serious way.

☐ **joyful**
TR 10

☐ **fun**
TR 11

☐ **celebrate**
TR 12

☐ **jolly**
☐ **merry**
TR 13 and TR 14

Check Your Understanding

A. Choose the sentence that correctly uses the underlined word.

1. a. Edward had lots of <u>fun</u> when he went to the beach last summer.
   b. Edward had lots of <u>fun</u> while he was taking his final exams.

2. a. Glenda is <u>glad</u> to go to the dentist after such a long time.
   b. Glenda is <u>glad</u> to see her best friend after such a long time.

3. a. I am so <u>happy</u> that you could come to my party.
   b. I am so <u>happy</u> that you are sick.

4. a. Paul told a really funny <u>joke</u> that made everyone laugh.
   b. Paul told a very serious <u>joke</u> during his speech.

5. a. Mr. Peterson is so <u>jolly</u>. He's always smiling and laughing.
   b. Mr. Peterson is so <u>jolly</u>. He's always complaining and yelling.

6. a. The loss of their dog has brought so much <u>joy</u> to that family.
   b. The baby has brought so much <u>joy</u> to that family.

7. a. The teacher was <u>merry</u> after all her students failed the test.
   b. The teacher was <u>merry</u> when it was time for vacation.

8. a. At recess, the students go out to <u>play</u> in the schoolyard.
   b. In the library, the students <u>play</u> with their schoolwork.

9. a. I am certain that these bad grades will <u>please</u> my mother.
   b. I am certain that these flowers will <u>please</u> my mother.

10. a. Timmy is a very <u>silly</u> boy. He is always reading books.
    b. Timmy is a very <u>silly</u> boy. He is always telling jokes.

11. a. What should we do to <u>celebrate</u> your new job?
    b. What should we do to <u>celebrate</u> the robbery?

12. a. It brings me great <u>happiness</u> to win the award.
    b. It brings me great <u>happiness</u> to have a cold.

13. a. Mary is never smiling and has a good sense of <u>humor</u>.
    b. Mary is always laughing and has a good sense of <u>humor</u>.

14. a. It was a <u>joyful</u> day when I broke my leg.
    b. It was a <u>joyful</u> day when my kitten was born.

B. Write **T** for **true statements** and **F** for **false statements**.

1. _____ When people are at a party, they are probably having fun.

2. _____ If you are glad to see somebody, you wish that they had not come.

3. _____ If somebody brings you a present, it may make you happy.

4. _____ When you tell a joke, you want to make somebody laugh.

5. _____ A person who is jolly is always crying.

6. _____ You will probably feel joy if you fight with a friend.

7. _____ If somebody tells you to have a merry time, they want you to be happy.

8. _____ Your teachers like it when you are playing during an exam.

9. _____ If you want to please your parents, you should disobey them.

10. _____ If a child acts silly, she probably wants to make you laugh.

11. _____ You might celebrate your birthday by having a party.

12. _____ After a car accident, you will probably feel a lot of happiness.

13. _____ A person with a good sense of humor usually does not like jokes.

14. _____ A graduation is an example of a joyful event.

Challenge Words

Check (✔) the words you already know.

☐ amuse   ☐ delight   ☐ glee   ☐ playful

☐ cheerful   ☐ entertain   ☐ pamper   ☐ pleasure

55. Caring and Trusting

Check (✔) the words you already know. Then, listen and repeat.

Tracks 1–7

Check Your Understanding

A. Match each sentence in the first column with the correct situation in the second column. One situation will not be used.

1. _____ Mary believes her father.

2. _____ Mary gives her father care.

3. _____ Mary enjoys spending time with her father.

4. _____ Mary's father likes to read.

5. _____ Mary loves her father.

6. _____ Mary's father forgives her.

7. _____ Mary's father wants her to study.

a. Mary has done something wrong, but her father is no longer angry at her.

b. Mary's father has told her something, and she thinks it is true.

c. Mary and her father really like to take walks together.

d. Mary's father provides food and shelter for her.

e. Mary looked after her father when he had the flu.

f. Mary's father is happy when he has a book.

g. Mary's father feels a need for her to be successful at school.

h. Mary really cares for her father very much.

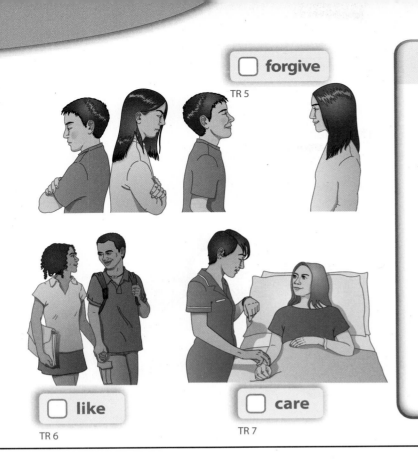

forgive

TR 5

like
TR 6

care
TR 7

Definitions

To **believe** someone means to feel sure that person is telling the truth.

Care is concern and kindness shown for others.

To **enjoy** means to like doing something.

To **forgive** someone who has done something bad or wrong means to stop being angry with that person.

To **like** means to think that an object or a person is interesting, enjoyable, or attractive.

To **love** means to care very much about someone, or to have strong romantic feelings for them.

To **want** means to feel a need for something.

B. Choose the correct word from the word bank to complete each sentence.

care	like	loves	wants
believe	enjoys	forgive	

1. My sister really _____ to go to Florida with her friends next month.

2. I really _____ to cook. I make dinner every night of the week.

3. Anna is a babysitter and takes _____ of small children while their parents are at work.

4. Olivia told me that she was not afraid of the dark woods, but I did not _____ her.

5. It was hard for Regina to _____ her friend Adam after he forgot her birthday.

6. I know that my sister _____ me and cares for me very much.

7. I think that Grandma really _____ going out to tea with her friends.

Challenge Words

Check (✔) the words you already know.

☐ admire   ☐ appreciate   ☐ depend   ☐ prefer   ☐ respect

☐ affection   ☐ approve   ☐ gratitude   ☐ regret   ☐ value

291. Fear

Check (✔) the words you already know. Then, listen and repeat.

Tracks 1–4

☐ **afraid**

TR 1

☐ **alarm**
☐ **fear**

TR 2 and TR 3

Check Your Understanding

A. Complete the story with the correct word from the word bank.

afraid	alarm	fears	nervous

Last night, there was a big storm. My brother is very (1) _____ of storms. Thunder is one of his biggest _____. When the rain started, he became (2) _____. He went to his bedroom and hid under the covers, but the loud thunder made him yell out in (3) _____. He stayed hidden in his room until the storm stopped.

☐ **nervous**

TR 4

Definitions

When you are **afraid** to do something, you are frightened because you think that something very unpleasant is going to happen to you.

Alarm is a feeling of fear or anxiety that something unpleasant or dangerous might happen.

Fear is the unpleasant feeling that you have when you think that you are in danger.

When you are **nervous**, you are frightened or worried.

B. Underline the correct word to complete each sentence.

1. The news that a major storm was coming caused (**afraid / alarm**) in the town.

2. I did not know that Pat was (**afraid / alarm**) of spiders.

3. My biggest (**fear / nervous**) is losing my dog.

4. Are you (**fear / nervous**) when you speak in front of a large group of people?

Challenge Words

Check (✔) the words you already know.

☐ dread   ☐ frantic   ☐ horror   ☐ shock

☐ eerie   ☐ fright   ☐ panic   ☐ terror

45

292. Anger

Check (✔) the words you already know. Then, listen and repeat.

Tracks 1–5

☐ **angry**
☐ **mad**

TR 1 and TR 2

☐ **dislike**

TR 3

☐ **anger**

TR 4

Check Your Understanding

A. Choose the sentence that correctly uses the underlined word.

1. a. I could hear the <u>anger</u> in my mother's voice when I told her I lost her favorite necklace.

   b. I could hear the <u>anger</u> in my mother's voice when I gave her a birthday present.

2. a. When she finds out that you bought her a nice vase, Mom will be <u>angry</u>.

   b. When she finds out that you broke her favorite vase, Mom will be <u>angry</u>.

3. a. Most people really <u>dislike</u> getting a tooth pulled.

   b. Most people really <u>dislike</u> buying freshly cut flowers.

4. a. I really <u>hate</u> the sound of my alarm when it goes off at 5:00 A.M.

   b. I really <u>hate</u> the sound of my favorite song on my MP3 player.

5. a. Are you <u>mad</u> that your favorite team won the game?

   b. Are you <u>mad</u> that I did not go to the game with you?

□ **hate**

TR 5

Definitions

Anger is the strong emotion that you feel when someone has behaved badly or has treated you unfairly.

When you are **angry**, you feel a strong dislike for something.

When you **dislike** something, you think that it is unpleasant, and you do not like it.

To **hate** means to have a strong feeling of dislike for something.

When someone is **mad**, that person is very angry.

B. Write **T** for **true statements** and **F** for **false statements**.

1. _____ When you feel anger, you probably do not smile.

2. _____ If somebody stole your money, you might get angry.

3. _____ If you dislike something, you want a lot of it.

4. _____ When somebody hates you, he wants to spend all his time with you.

5. _____ If you come to class late every day, your teacher might get mad.

Challenge Words

Check (✔) the words you already know.

□ disgust □ hatred □ irritate □ rage □ revenge

□ fury □ hostile □ offend □ resent □ temper

47

293. Desire

Check (✔) the words you already know. Then, listen and repeat.

Tracks 1–6

☐ **expect**

TR 1

☐ **need**

TR 2

☐ **want**

TR 3

Check Your Understanding

A. Choose the correct word from the word bank to complete each sentence.

miss	needs	want
expects	selfish	wishes

1. After a long day, your body _____ a good night's sleep.

2. I cannot wait until Angela comes back from her trip. I really _____ her.

3. Do you _____ to take Spanish lessons with me next year?

4. Marianne _____ she could go to Europe, but she does not have the money now.

5. Martha _____ her son to be home very soon.

6. Please don't be so _____. Share with everyone else!

selfish
TR 4

wish
TR 5

miss
TR 6

Definitions

To **expect** means to think that something will happen or something will come.

When you **miss** someone who is not with you, you feel sad that they are not there.

When you **need** something, you must have it.

Someone who is **selfish** cares only about themselves and not about other people.

To **want** means to feel a desire or need for something.

To **wish** for something means to hope that it will happen.

B. Underline the correct word to complete each sentence.

1. How many copies do we (**need** / **miss**) so that each student has one?

2. It's 6:00. Amy (**expects** / **misses**) her husband to arrive home any minute.

3. Sometimes, I really (**expect** / **miss**) Ms. Stone. She left our school last year.

4. Did you ever (**wish** / **need**) that you could travel to outer space?

5. Nicole always helps other people and is never (**expecting** / **selfish**).

6. Teddy never (**wants** / **expects**) to play with other children. He likes to be alone.

Challenge Words

Check (✔) the words you already know.

- [ ] anticipate
- [ ] desire
- [ ] hanker
- [ ] yearn
- [ ] crave
- [ ] greed
- [ ] seek

311. Cruelty and Meanness

Check (✔) the words you already know. Then, listen and repeat.

Tracks 1–4

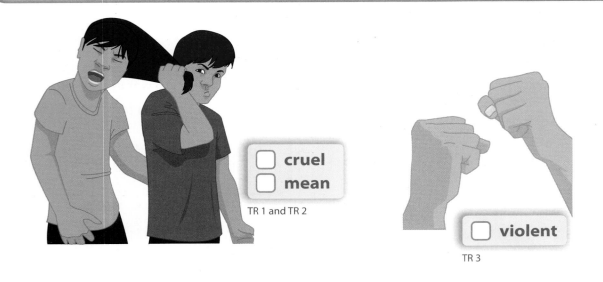

☐ **cruel**
☐ **mean**

TR 1 and TR 2

☐ **violent**

TR 3

Check Your Understanding

A. Circle the best example of each word.

1. mean

   a. not petting your dog for two days because he chewed up your slippers

   b. taking your dog to the vetrinarian for a check up

2. cruel

   a. calling one of your classmates "pretty and smart"

   b. calling one of your classmates "ugly and stupid"

3. unkind

   a. telling your mother that you love her

   b. telling your mother that you do not love her

4. violent

   a. hugging and holding hands with another person

   b. kicking and punching something

Definitions

Someone who is **cruel** purposely makes people suffer.

Someone who is **mean** is unkind or cruel.

Someone who is **unkind** behaves in an unpleasant and unfriendly way.

Someone who is **violent** or does something **violent** uses physical force to hurt other people.

☐ unkind

TR 4

B. Write **T** for **true statements** and **F** for **false statements**.

1. _____ If your parents do not give you dessert after dinner, they are being cruel to you.

2. _____ Someone who is angry and yells might be mean to you.

3. _____ It is unkind to tell your friend that she did well in her dance performance.

4. _____ A person who always wants to hit something is violent.

Challenge Words

Check (✔) the words you already know.

☐ cruelty ☐ drastic ☐ fierce ☐ savage

☐ destructive ☐ ferocious ☐ merciless ☐ vicious

312. General Upset

Check (✔) the words you already know. Then, listen and repeat.

☐ **upset**

TR 1

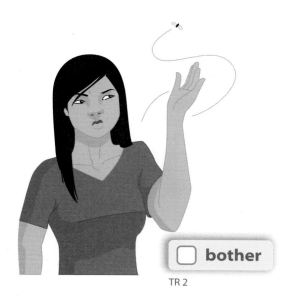

☐ **bother**

TR 2

Check Your Understanding

A. Choose the correct word from the word bank to complete each sentence.

alone	upset	bothering

1. I could not sleep because my neighbor's loud music was _____ me.

2. I am going to visit my grandpa so he doesn't feel _____ this weekend.

3. James _____ his little brother by telling him a scary story.

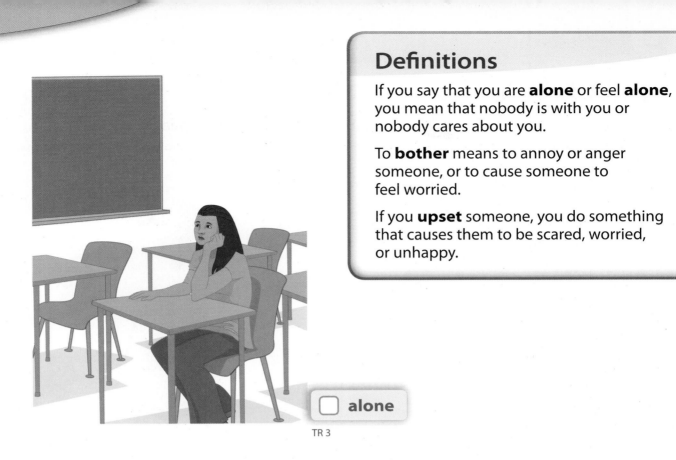

☐ **alone**

TR 3

B. Write **T** for **true statements** and **F** for **false statements**.

1. _____ If you are alone, you always have a lot of people around you.

2. _____ When something bothers you, you find it pleasant and enjoyable.

3. _____ Being away from your friends for a long time might upset you.

Challenge Words

Check (✔) the words you already know.

☐ dejected   ☐ disappoint   ☐ distress   ☐ frustrate   ☐ serious

☐ depress   ☐ discourage   ☐ disturb   ☐ impose   ☐ solemn

313. Doubt and Hope

Check (✔) the words you already know. Then, listen and repeat.

I don't think I will win.

I will win this race.

☐ **belief**
TR 2

☐ **doubt**
TR 1

☐ **hope**
TR 3

Check Your Understanding

A. Choose the correct word from the word bank to complete each sentence.

beliefs	doubts	hope	trust

1. Joseph's project is due tomorrow and he has _____ about whether he can finish it on time.

2. Do you have strong _____ about how the school should be run?

3. Michael has _____ in his assistant, on whom he relies to do a good job.

4. Yvette lost _____ of winning the tournament when she dropped the ball.

trust

TR 4

Definitions

Belief is a powerful feeling that something is real or true.

If you have **doubt** or **doubts** about something, you do not feel certain about it.

Hope is the feeling of wanting something good to happen and believing that it will.

Trust is the belief that a person is honest and that they will not knowingly do harm.

B. Match each word to the best example. One example will not be used.

1. _____ belief

2. _____ hope

3. _____ doubt

4. _____ trust

a. You knew the weekend would be sunny, so you planned a picnic.

b. Your friend says she is going to make you a sweater, but you think she will never finish it.

c. You practice very hard during your skating lessons. Maybe one day you will be a professional skater.

d. You feel very strongly that you are the best person for the job.

e. Your parents give you the secret code to their debit card for emergencies.

Challenge Words

Check (✔) the words you already know.

☐ despair

☐ desperate

☐ disappointment

☐ faith

☐ hopeless

☐ optimism

378. Guilt and Worry

Check (✔) the words you already know. Then, listen and repeat.

Tracks 1–3

- ☐ **guilt**
- ☐ **shame**

TR 1 and TR 2

Check Your Understanding

A. Choose the correct word from the box to complete each sentence.

guilt	shame	worry

1. Sara felt such _____ after Mr. Smith heard her say she did not like his class.

2. Madeleine is out of a job, and she cannot pay her rent. She really has a lot of things to _____ about right now.

3. Ken felt a lot of _____ after he lost his little brother's favorite toy.

Definitions

Guilt is an unhappy feeling that you have when you think that you have done something wrong.

Shame is the very uncomfortable feeling that you have when you have done something wrong or embarrassing.

Worry is the feeling of anxiety and unhappiness caused by thinking about unpleasant things that might happen.

☐ **worry**

TR 3

B. Match each word to the best example. One example will not be used.

1. _____ guilt

2. _____ shame

3. _____ worry

a. When Adam missed school two days in a row, his teacher called his house to make sure he was all right.

b. Jake felt so silly when he forgot his speech in front of the whole class.

c. Sherri picked some flowers from her garden and gave them to her neighbor.

d. Ida feels terrible about lying to her friend.

Challenge Words

Check (✔) the words you already know.

☐ anxiety   ☐ concern   ☐ suspense   ☐ uncomfortable

☐ anxious   ☐ humiliation   ☐ tense   ☐ uneasy

379. Irritability

Check (✔) the words you already know. Then, listen and repeat.

Tracks 1–3

□ **grumpy**

TR 1

□ **rude**

TR 2

Check Your Understanding

A. Circle the correct word to complete each sentence.

1. If you cut in front of three other people who have been waiting in line, you are being _____.

   a. a grouch

   b. grumpy

   c. rude

2. If you are normally a happy person but you feel a little annoyed today, you are _____.

   a. grouch

   b. grumpy

   c. rude

3. If an adult yells at children for no reason and never smiles, he could be _____.

   a. a grouch

   b. grumpy

   c. rude

☐ **grouch**

TR 3

Definitions

A **grouch** is someone who always complains.

When someone is **grumpy**, that person is a little angry.

When a person is **rude**, he or she does or says something that is unkind or impolite.

B. Match each word to the correct description. One description will not be used.

1. _____ grouch
2. _____ grumpy
3. _____ rude

a. unkind or impolite actions

b. to say something in an unhappy way

c. someone who is always in a bad mood

d. a little angry

Challenge Words

Check (✔) the words you already know.

☐ disagreeable   ☐ gruff   ☐ grumble

380. Excitement and Attention

Check (✔) the words you already know. Then, listen and repeat.

Tracks 1–3

☐ amaze

TR 1

☐ surprise

TR 2

Check Your Understanding

A. Circle the correct answer.

1. Which of the following would amaze you the most?

   a. seeing a tiger walk through your house

   b. watching your favorite television program

   c. doing your homework

2. Which of the following would excite you the most?

   a. having three exams in one day

   b. winning $1 million

   c. eating a hamburger

3. Which of the following would surprise you the most?

   a. if your teacher gave you homework

   b. if your teacher sat down to eat lunch in the middle of class

   c. if your teacher asked a student to sit down

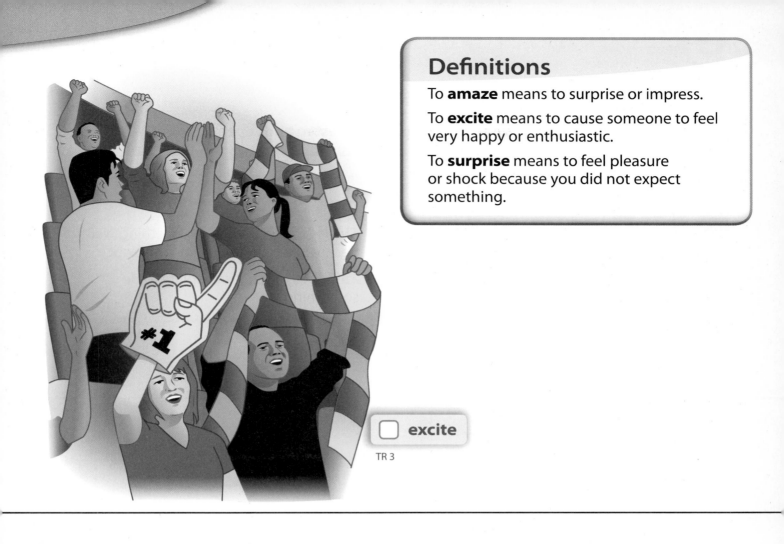

Definitions

To **amaze** means to surprise or impress.

To **excite** means to cause someone to feel very happy or enthusiastic.

To **surprise** means to feel pleasure or shock because you did not expect something.

☐ **excite**

TR 3

B. Choose the sentence that correctly uses the underlined word.

1. a. I am <u>amazed</u> that Anne went to the party with you. She never goes out.

   b. I am <u>amazed</u> that Anne went to the party with you. You two are always together.

2. a. The trip to the doctor's office <u>excited</u> the children.

   b. The trip to the zoo <u>excited</u> the children.

3. a. I was <u>surprised</u> to see my teacher at the movies.

   b. I was <u>surprised</u> to see my teacher in the classroom.

Challenge Words

Check (✔) the words you already know.

☐ amazement   ☐ astonish   ☐ awe   ☐ marvel   ☐ rejoice

☐ appall   ☐ astonishment   ☐ disbelief   ☐ passion   ☐ thrill

381. General Human Traits

Check (✔) the words you already know. Then, listen and repeat.

☐ **talent**

TR 2

☐ **skill**

TR 1

Definitions

Skill is the ability to do something well because of training, talent, or practice.

Talent is your natural ability to do something well.

Check Your Understanding

A. Circle the phrase that is the best example of each word.

1. skill

   a. the ability to read a very difficult text   b. the ability to go to sleep before ten o'clock

2. talent

   a. the ability to throw something away   b. the ability to sing very well

3. skill

   a. the inability to do a task well   b. the ability to do a task very well

B. Write **T** for **true statements** and **F** for **false statements**.

1. _____ When you work very hard to do something, and you still do not do it well, it shows you have talent.

2. _____ If you have good writing skills, you are able to write well.

3. _____ You do not have to practice to develop a skill.

4. _____ If you have talent as a chef, people do not usually like the food you make.

Challenge Words

Check (✔) the words you already know.

☐ attitude   ☐ discipline   ☐ knack   ☐ personality

☐ capacity   ☐ feature   ☐ manner   ☐ quality

416. Actions Related to Fear

Check (✔) the word if you already know it. Then, listen and repeat.

Track 1

☐ **scare**

TR 1

Definition

To **scare** means to cause fear or to frighten someone.

Check Your Understanding

A. Check (✔) each thing that might **scare** you.

☐ having a friend jump out at you in the dark

☐ losing a game of checkers

☐ getting lost in the forest

☐ not being able to swim in the deep end of a swimming pool

☐ being in the park with your family on a sunny afternoon

B. Choose the sentence that correctly uses the underlined word.

1. a. The large, angry dog <u>scared</u> Maggie.

   b. Anita was <u>scared</u> when she saw that she did very well on the test.

2. a. When Arnold saw his grandmother, he was <u>scared</u> and gave her a big hug.

   b. The boys <u>scared</u> the birds away.

3. a. Being in an airplane really <u>scares</u> my mother.

   b. Did you <u>scare</u> the book?

Challenge Words

Check (✔) the words you already know.

☐ cringe   ☐ haunt   ☐ petrify   ☐ terrify

☐ flinch   ☐ horrify   ☐ startle   ☐ wince

63

417. Envy and Jealousy

Check (✔) the word if you already know it. Then, listen and repeat.

Track 1

Definition

When you are **jealous** of another person's possessions or qualities, you feel angry because you do not have those possessions or qualities.

☐ **jealous**

TR 1

Check Your Understanding

A. Check (✔) the examples of a person who is **jealous**.

☐ Marc is angry that Jon caught a big fish and he did not.

☐ Betty really loves to spend time with her little sister at the museum.

☐ Tim worked really hard to get a good part in the play, so he was upset when Rob got the lead part and he didn't.

☐ You have such a beautiful home. I wish I had a home as nice as yours.

☐ Peter and Mike congratulated each other after their team won the game.

B. Write **T** for **true statements** and **F** for **false statements**.

1. _____ You are happy when you are jealous.

2. _____ You are jealous if you are upset because someone has something that you don't have.

3. _____ You are not jealous if you are happy with what you have.

Challenge Words

Check (✔) the words you already know.

☐ envy   ☐ grudge   ☐ jealousy   ☐ possessive

151. Facial Expressions

Check (✔) the words you already know. Then, listen and repeat.

Tracks 1–4

☐ **nod**

TR 1

Definitions

A **frown** is an expression that you make by moving your eyebrows and mouth downward to show that you are upset or concentrating.

A **grin** is a big smile.

A **nod** is an up and down movement of the head to show that you agree with something.

A **smile** is an expression that you make by moving the corners of your mouth upward to show that you are happy or think something is funny.

☐ **frown**

TR 2

☐ **grin**

TR 3

☐ **smile**

TR 4

Check Your Understanding

A. Underline the correct word to complete each sentence.

1. I could tell by the (**grin** / **frown**) on his face that Sam was in a good mood.

2. Grandma was laughing at the joke, so she had a (**frown** / **smile**) on her face.

3. I saw your father (**frown** / **nod**) at you. I'm glad that he gave you permission to go to the movies.

4. I don't want to bother Eva right now. She must be thinking very hard about something, because she has a (**frown** / **smile**) on her face.

B. Circle the correct answer to complete each sentence.

1. You might wear a *grin* if _____ .

   a. your friend tells you she just got a new job

   b. your mom tells you that you must take out the trash

   c. you are working very hard at something

2. You might show a *smile* if _____ .

   a. you get an F on your report card

   b. you get a funny text message from a friend

   c. you lose your favorite book

3. You might show a *frown* if _____ .

   a. you are trying to understand something in another language

   b. you are excited to see your family

   c. you are eating an ice cream cone

4. You might give a *nod* if _____ .

   a. you don't want your little brother using your computer

   b. you don't agree with what your friend is saying

   c. you let your cousins play with your new video game

Challenge Words

Check (✔) the words you already know.

☐ blush ☐ scowl ☐ smirk ☐ sneer

152. Actions Associated with the Mouth

Check (✔) the words you already know. Then, listen and repeat.

 Tracks 1–4

☐ **suck**
TR 1

Definitions

To **kiss** someone means to touch them with your lips to show love or to greet them.

When you **lick** something, you move your tongue across its surface.

To **spit** means to force a small amount of food or liquid out of your mouth.

When you **suck** a liquid, you use your lips to bring the liquid to your mouth.

☐ **kiss**
TR 3

☐ **lick**
TR 2

☐ **spit**
TR 4

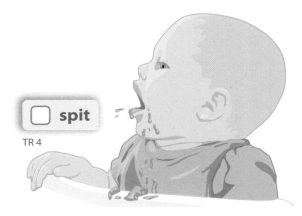

Check Your Understanding

A. Match each word to the correct situation below. One situation will not be used.

1. _____ kiss
2. _____ suck
3. _____ lick
4. _____ spit

a. a drink you do not like
b. a chocolate milkshake
c. your grandmother
d. an ice cream cone
e. a candle to put it out

B. Underline the correct word to complete each sentence.

1. The cat (**licked / kissed**) its paws to clean them.

2. The baby will (**suck / lick**) from the bottle when she is hungry.

3. After biting into a rotten piece of fruit, she (**kissed / spit**) it into a napkin.

4. Louie's sister always greets him by (**kissing / spitting**) him.

Challenge Words

Check (✔) the word if you already know it.

☐ spew

196. Breathing

Check (✔) the words you already know. Then, listen and repeat.

 Tracks 1–4

☐ choke
TR 1

Definitions

To **blow** means to send out air from your mouth.

Your **breath** is the air that you let out through your mouth when you breathe.

To **choke** means that you cannot breathe because you do not have enough air, or because something is blocking your throat.

To **exhale** means to breathe air out of your body.

☐ breath
TR 3

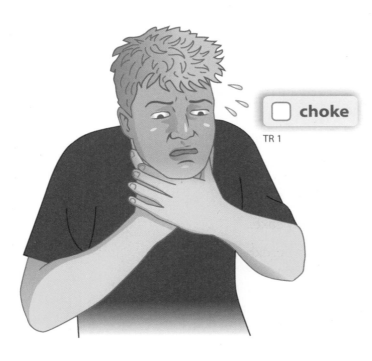

☐ blow
TR 2

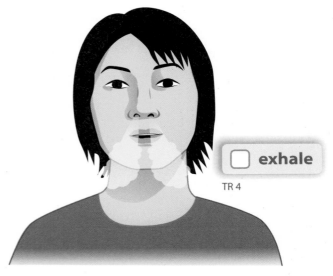

☐ exhale
TR 4

Check Your Understanding

A. Write T for true statements and F for false statements.

1. _____ You might make something move by blowing on it.

2. _____ Your breath is air that you let out of your mouth when you breathe.

3. _____ When you choke on something, you send air out from your mouth.

4. _____ When you exhale, you take air into your body.

B. Circle the correct word to complete each sentence.

1. Ellie _____ for the doctor while he listened to her heart.

    a. breath   b. choked   c. exhaled

2. I could see my _____ when I walked outside in the cold weather.

    a. breath   b. blow   c. choke

3. Grandpa has a lot of candles to _____ out on his birthday cake.

    a. breath   b. blow   c. exhale

4. Don't eat too fast. You might _____ .

    a. blow   b. choke   c. exhale

Challenge Words

Check (✔) the words you already know.

☐ pant   ☐ puff   ☐ respire   ☐ strangle   ☐ whiff

241. Actions Associated with the Nose

Check (✔) the words you already know. Then, listen and repeat.

Tracks 1–6

☐ **smell**

TR 1

☐ **sneeze**

TR 2

Definitions

To **smell** means to sense an odor when you breathe through your nose.

To **sneeze** means to send air forcefully through your nose and mouth because of an irritation or cold.

To **sniff** means to breathe in air through your nose, often suddenly or quickly.

To **snore** means to make sounds from your nose and mouth while you are sleeping.

To **snort** means to breathe air noisily out through the nose.

Stink is a bad smell.

☐ **snort**

TR 4

☐ **sniff**

TR 3

☐ **stink**

TR 6

☐ **snore**

TR 5

Check Your Understanding

A. Write **T** for **true statements** and **F** for **false statements**.

1. _____ You need your eyes to smell.

2. _____ If you sneeze, you might have a cold.

3. _____ A dog might sniff your hand to see if he knows you.

4. _____ People usually snore when they are awake.

5. _____ When you snort, you breathe air noisily from your nose.

6. _____ Fresh roses will create a stink in your home.

B. Circle the correct word to complete each sentence.

1. Many people _____ when they are sick.

   a. snort   b. smell   c. sneeze

2. Billy left milk in his locker over the weekend, and now there is a very bad _____ in the hall.

   a. snort   b. stink   c. sneeze

3. My wife says I _____ in my sleep, but I know I don't!

   a. smell   b. sniff   c. snore

4. I love to _____ cookies baking in the oven.

   a. smell   b. snort   c. snore

5. At the zoo, we watched the hippo as it _____ water through its nose.

   a. sniffed   b. snored   c. snorted

6. Pam _____ the cheese to see if it was still good to eat.

   a. sniffed   b. snored   c. snorted

Challenge Words

Check (✔) the words you already know.

☐ aroma   ☐ fume   ☐ odor   ☐ reek   ☐ stench

☐ fragrant   ☐ inhale   ☐ perfume   ☐ scent

92. Fasteners

Check (✔) the words you already know. Then, listen and repeat.

Tracks 1–14

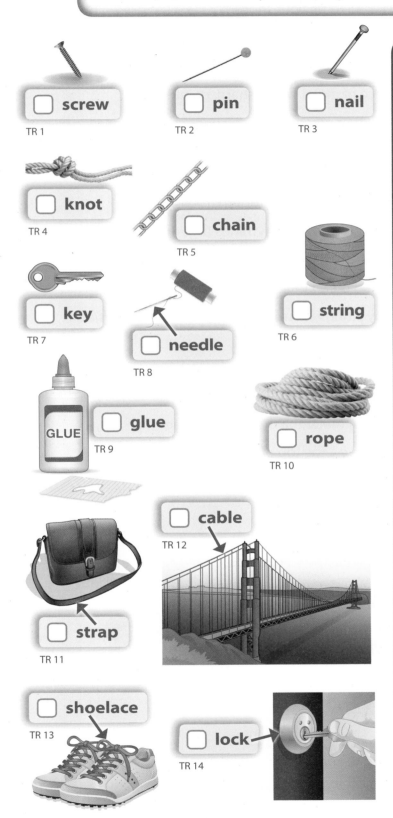

☐ screw
TR 1

☐ pin
TR 2

☐ nail
TR 3

☐ knot
TR 4

☐ chain
TR 5

☐ key
TR 7

☐ needle
TR 8

☐ string
TR 6

☐ glue
TR 9

☐ rope
TR 10

☐ cable
TR 12

☐ strap
TR 11

☐ shoelace
TR 13

☐ lock
TR 14

Definitions

A **cable** is a very strong, thick rope made of metal that holds or fastens heavy objects.

A **chain** is a line of metal rings that are connected together.

Glue is a sticky substance used for joining things together.

A **key** is a specially shaped piece of metal that opens or closes a lock.

A **knot** is made when you tie two pieces of string or rope together.

The **lock** on a door or a container is the part that you use to keep it shut and to make sure that no one can open it. You can open a lock with a key.

A **nail** is a thin piece of metal with one pointed end and one flat end. You hit the flat end with a hammer to push the nail into a wall.

A **needle** is a small, thin metal tool with a sharp point that you use for sewing.

A **pin** is a very small, thin piece of metal with a point at one end that holds items together.

A **rope** is a type of very thick string that is made by twisting together several smaller strings.

A **screw** is a small, grooved metal object with a sharp end that you use to join things together.

A **shoelace** is a long, thick string that you use to fasten your shoes.

A **strap** is a long, narrow piece of leather or other material.

String is thin rope that is made out of twisted threads.

Check Your Understanding

A. Match each word to the correct description. One description will not be used.

1. _____ chain
2. _____ glue
3. _____ key
4. _____ lock
5. _____ nail
6. _____ needle
7. _____ pin
8. _____ rope
9. _____ string
10. _____ cable
11. _____ knot
12. _____ screw
13. _____ shoelace
14. _____ strap

a. a long string that is used to tie your shoes

b. two pieces of rope or string tied together

c. a set of threads twisted together that used to tie things

d. a very small, thin piece of metal with a sharp, pointed end

e. a small piece of metal that you hammer to connect two pieces of wood

f. a small metal item that opens a door's lock

g. a series of metal rings that are joined together

h. a sticky substance that you use to join things together

i. a metal object that you open with a key

j. a small piece of pointed metal that is used for sewing

k. a thick group of many strings twisted together that is used to tie things down

l. an opening in a lock in which a key goes

m. a strong, thick rope made of metal

n. a small, grooved piece of metal that holds things together

o. a leather or cloth handle on the top of a purse or suitcase

B. Circle the correct item that you would use in each situation.

1. You get into the car and put on your seatbelt.

   a. screws   b. knots   c. straps

2. You are building a bridge for your science project.

   a. string   b. cable   c. chain

3. You do not want anyone to go in your room while you are out.

   a. lock   b. nail   c. needle

4. You want to hold two pieces of cloth together so you can sew them.

   a. rope   b. glue   c. pin

5. You have a cardboard box that you do not want to come open.

   a. screw   b. string   c. chain

6. You want to leave your bike outside while you go into the store.

   a. chain   b. nail   c. screw

7. You want to hammer two boards together to make a birdhouse.

   a. pin   b. nail   c. strap

8. You have a hole in your shirt, and you want to sew it.

   a. needle   b. glue   c. key

9. You broke the handle off your favorite mug, and you want to put it back on.

   a. screw   b. knot   c. glue

10. You want to go into your house, but the door is locked.

   a. shoelace   b. chain   c. key

11. You have a new swing, and you want to hang it from a tree in the yard.

   a. rope   b. shoelace   c. key

12. You want to fix a broken chair.

   a. screw   b. pin   c. key

13. You want to go running, and you are putting your shoes on.

   a. glue   b. shoelace   c. cable

14. You don't want your shoelaces to come loose while you are running.

   a. chain   b. knot   c. rope

Challenge Words

Check (✔) the words you already know.

☐ bolt   ☐ hinge   ☐ latch   ☐ slot   ☐ tack

☐ clamp   ☐ keyhole   ☐ padlock   ☐ staple   ☐ twine

96. Cooking and Eating Utensils

Check (✔) the words you already know. Then, listen and repeat.

 Tracks 1–16

☐ **dish**
☐ **plate**

TR 1 and TR 2

☐ **pan**

TR 3

☐ **pot**

TR 8

☐ **tray**

TR 9

☐ **bowl**

TR 12

☐ **opener**

TR 13

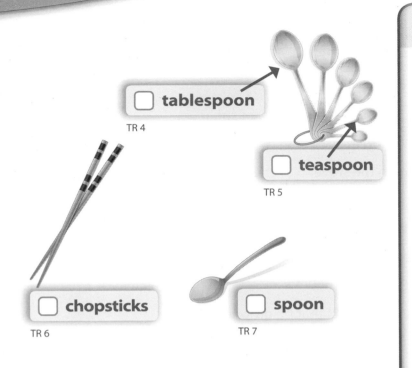

☐ **tablespoon**
TR 4

☐ **teaspoon**
TR 5

☐ **chopsticks**
TR 6

☐ **spoon**
TR 7

☐ **knife**
TR 10

☐ **fork**
TR 11

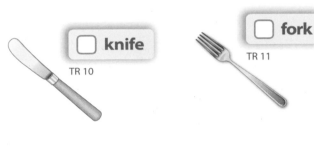

☐ **mug**
TR 14

☐ **glass**
TR 15

☐ **cup**
TR 16

Definitions

A **bowl** is a round container that is used for mixing and serving food.

Chopsticks are thin sticks of wood or plastic that some people use to pick up and eat food.

A **cup** is a small, round, open container that you drink from.

A **dish** is a plate, bowl, or other container used to serve and hold food.

A **fork** is a tool for eating, with a handle and two or more long points to pick up food.

A **glass** is a container made from glass, which you can drink from.

A **knife** is a sharp, flat piece of metal with a handle that can be used to cut things.

A **mug** is a deep cup with a handle, which you can drink hot liquids from.

An **opener** is a tool that is used for opening cans or bottles.

A **pan** is a round metal container with a long handle that you use for cooking things in.

A **plate** is a flat dish that is used to hold food.

A **pot** is a deep, round container used for cooking food.

A **spoon** is a long object with a round end used for eating, serving, or mixing food.

A **tablespoon** is a large spoon that you use to measure ingredients when you are cooking.

A **teaspoon** is a small spoon that you use for putting sugar into tea or coffee. It is smaller than a tablespoon.

A **tray** is a flat piece of wood, plastic, or metal that is used for carrying things, especially food and drinks.

Check Your Understanding

A. Underline the correct word to complete each sentence.

1. The recipe says that we need to add three (**mugs / tablespoons**) of sugar.

2. Have you ever tried eating with (**openers / chopsticks**)?

3. There is a large (**tray / pot**) of water boiling on the stove.

4. If you want to eat that ice cream, you are going to need a (**knife / spoon**).

5. Sara put the cooked turkey in a large, white (**dish / knife**).

6. Sometimes, nothing tastes better than a cold (**bowl / glass**) of lemonade.

7. I put some oil in the (**knife / pan**) to cook the vegetables.

8. There were so many plates on the waiter's (**tray / fork**) that he dropped it.

9. Do you have a (**plate / teaspoon**) that I could use to stir my coffee?

10. The mother called her children to come in from the cold for a (**fork / mug**) of hot chocolate.

11. Please try to keep your food on your (**opener / plate**), and off the table!

12. Sally poured a (**tray / cup**) of juice for her son.

13. Except for sandwiches, I eat most of my food with a (**glass / fork**).

14. Maggie ordered a (**bowl / spoon**) of soup and a salad.

15. Use this (**cup / opener**) to take the lid off of the can of peaches.

16. The (**pan / knife**) on the table is for cutting your meat.

B. Circle the correct word to complete each sentence.

1. At the party, Mary served the fruit punch in colorful plastic _____ .

   a. openers   b. trays   c. cups

2. Mom cut a slice of cherry pie and put it into a blue _____ .

   a. mug   b. teaspoon   c. dish

3. Since I love coffee so much, my friend bought me this nice _____ .

   a. tray   b. mug   c. bowl

4. You cannot just twist the cap off. You need a bottle _____ .

   a. opener   b. glass   c. pot

5. Please put these _____ on the table for dinner.

   a. trays   b. plates   c. pots

6. The chef cooked the chicken in a _____ on the stove.

    a. pan   b. spoon   c. glass

7. I always eat with _____ when I am in a Chinese restaurant.

    a. spoons   b. chopsticks   c. knives

8. When I feel sick, my mother makes a _____ of chicken soup for me.

    a. teaspoon   b. knife   c. pot

9. When you set the table, please be sure to include a fork, knife, and _____ for each person.

    a. pan   b. opener   c. spoon

10. People can sometimes eat food with their hands, but usually they eat using a knife and _____.

    a. fork   b. teaspoon   c. mug

11. Luis is eating a _____ of chocolate ice cream.

    a. tray   b. knife   c. bowl

12. Please be careful that the _____ on your _____ do not fall and break.

    a. glasses / tray   b. knives / chopsticks   c. openers / pot

13. You need a sharp _____ to cut roast beef.

    a. pan   b. cup   c. knife

14. The cake needs more sugar than salt. The recipe calls for four _____ of sugar, but just a half _____ of salt.

    a. teaspoons / mug   b. trays / tablespoon   c. tablespoons / teaspoon

Challenge Words

Check (✔) the words you already know.

☐ casserole   ☐ kettle   ☐ platter   ☐ scoop   ☐ skillet

☐ goblet   ☐ ladle   ☐ saucer   ☐ silverware   ☐ spatula

118. Appliances

Check (✔) the words you already know. Then, listen and repeat.

Tracks 1–7

☐ stove
TR 3

☐ oven
TR 4

☐ heater
TR 2

☐ refrigerator
TR 1

Check Your Understanding

A. Choose the best word from the word bank to complete each sentence.

oven	stove	heater	refrigerator
radio	television	furnace	

1. When we got chilly on the patio, Dean brought out a little electric _____ to warm us up.

2. I heard my favorite song on the _____ when I was in the car today.

3. Please set the _____ to 300° and put the meat in for two hours.

4. Our _____ is powered by gas, and it heats the whole house.

5. Billy looked in the _____ but did not find any milk.

6. There is an excellent movie on _____ tonight.

7. Reheat the peas on the _____ after you bake the chicken in the oven.

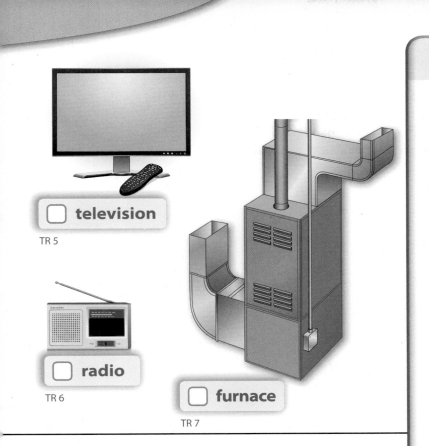

television

TR 5

radio

TR 6

furnace

TR 7

Definitions

A **furnace** is a large container that produces heat for a house or other living space.

A **heater** is a piece of equipment that heats water or air and makes a room warm.

An **oven** is a piece of equipment used for cooking, baking, and heating food.

A **radio** is a piece of equipment that you use in order to listen to radio programs.

A **refrigerator** is a large electric container that is used for keeping food cool.

A **stove** is a large piece of kitchen equipment, with electric or gas burners used to cook food.

A **television**, or **TV**, is a piece of electrical equipment with a screen that receives and shows moving pictures with sound.

B. Combine the phrases from each column to make logical sentences. One phrase in the second column will not be used.

1. _____ The smell of cookies baking ...

2. _____ The house was very cold because ...

3. _____ Can you please put a pot of water ...

4. _____ The only thing I watch on television ...

5. _____ My favorite song ...

6. _____ On a cold day, I need to ...

7. _____ There is plenty to eat ...

a. will cook faster in the microwave.

b. turn on the heater in my car.

c. is on the radio every day at 5:00 p.m.

d. is coming from the oven.

e. is the news.

f. in the refrigerator.

g. on the stove to boil?

h. the furnace was broken.

Challenge Words

Check (✔) the words you already know.

☐ griddle   ☐ kiln   ☐ phonograph   ☐ stereo

☐ icebox   ☐ microwave   ☐ radiator   ☐ wireless

119. Tools (General)

Check (✔) the words you already know. Then, listen and repeat.

Tracks 1–8

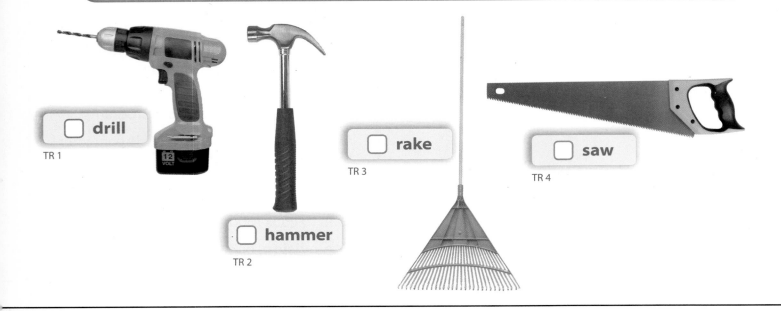

☐ **drill**

TR 1

☐ **hammer**

TR 2

☐ **rake**

TR 3

☐ **saw**

TR 4

Check Your Understanding

A. Circle the correct description for each word.

1. hammer
   a. a long, sharp metal object that you use to cut wood
   b. a piece of wood with a heavy metal end used to hit nails

2. saw
   a. a sharp metal object that you use to cut wood
   b. a small piece of metal that you squeeze together to move small objects

3. shovel
   a. a tool with a long handle that you use to move snow or dirt
   b. a piece of wood with a heavy metal end used to hit nails

4. tool
   a. any item that you use with your hands to make work easier
   b. an object with a long handle used to move snow or dirt

5. drill
   a. a garden tool with a long handle that is used to collect leaves and grass
   b. a tool that makes a hole in something

6. rake
   a. any item that you use with your hands to make work easier
   b. a garden tool with a long handle that is used to collect leaves and grass

7. screwdriver
   a. a long metal object that you turn to tighten things
   b. a piece of wood with a heavy metal end used to hit nails

8. tweezers
   a. a small piece of metal that you squeeze together to pick up small objects
   b. a tool with a long handle that you use to move snow or dirt

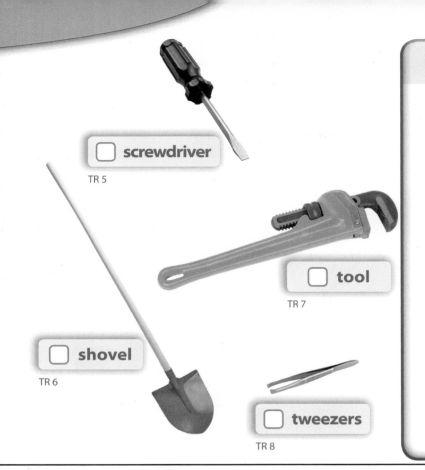

○ screwdriver
TR 5

○ tool
TR 7

○ shovel
TR 6

○ tweezers
TR 8

Definitions

A **drill** is a tool for making holes.

A **hammer** is a tool that is made from a heavy piece of metal attached to the end of a handle. It is used for hitting nails into wood.

A **rake** is a garden tool with a long handle, used for collecting loose grass or leaves.

A **saw** is a metal tool for cutting wood.

A **screwdriver** is a tool that you use for turning screws.

A **shovel** is a flat tool with a handle that is used for lifting and moving earth or snow.

A **tool** is anything that you hold in your hands and use to do a particular type of work.

Tweezers are a small tool that you use for picking up and removing small objects. Tweezers consist of two thin pieces of metal joined together at one end.

B. Circle the item that you would use for each task. Some tasks may have two items.

1. You want to build a tree house.	rake	hammer	tweezers
2. You want to cut a piece of wood.	saw	shovel	screwdriver
3. You want to hang something heavy on the wall.	saw	drill	tweezers
4. You want to make a birdhouse for your yard.	rake	tool	hammer
5. You want to plant an apple tree.	rake	shovel	screwdriver
6. You want to clean up leaves from your backyard.	saw	rake	screwdriver
7. You want to remove a wooden splinter from your foot.	tweezers	hammer	shovel
8. You just got a new bookcase, and you want to put it together.	tool	rake	screwdriver

Challenge Words

Check (✔) the words you already know.

○ chisel   ○ hoe   ○ lever   ○ resource   ○ utensil

○ device   ○ instrument   ○ pliers   ○ sandpaper   ○ wrench

83

163. Cutting Tools

Check (✔) the words you already know. Then, listen and repeat.

Tracks 1–6

☐ **axe**

TR 1

☐ **lawnmower**

TR 2

Check Your Understanding

A. Combine the phrases from each column to make logical sentences.

1. _____ Mark brought his pocketknife on the camping trip …

2. _____ I asked for a knife because …

3. _____ To chop some firewood, …

4. _____ The hairstylist needs …

5. _____ Please don't put your hand …

6. _____ Jack is getting the lawnmower out …

a. we first need to find an axe.

b. to sharpen the scissors before she cuts your hair.

c. so that he would be able to cut small sticks for the fire.

d. on the blade or you will get cut.

e. because the grass is too long.

f. I wanted to cut my sandwich in half.

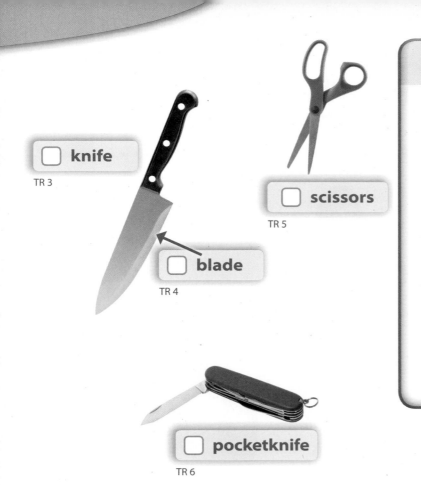

knife
TR 3

blade
TR 4

scissors
TR 5

pocketknife
TR 6

Definitions

An **axe** is a tool used for cutting wood. It has a heavy metal blade and a long handle.

The **blade** of a knife is the flat, sharp edge that is used for cutting.

A **knife** is a sharp, flat piece of metal with a handle, that you can use to cut things or use as a weapon.

A **lawnmower** is a machine used for cutting grass.

A **pocketknife** is a small knife with a blade that folds into the handle.

Scissors are a small tool for cutting with two sharp parts that are joined together.

B. Write **T** for **true statements** and **F** for **false statements**.

1. _____ If you want to chop a piece of wood, you can use an axe.

2. _____ It is always best to hold a knife by the blade.

3. _____ You use a lawnmower inside your house.

4. _____ A pocketknife folds up so that you may carry it safely.

5. _____ Scissors have two blades.

6. _____ People generally cut their hair with a knife.

Challenge Words

Check (✔) the words you already know.

- [ ] barb
- [ ] clipper
- [ ] hatchet
- [ ] jackknife
- [ ] razor
- [ ] scythe
- [ ] sickle
- [ ] straightedge

85

242. Abrasive / Cutting Actions

Check (✔) the words you already know. Then, listen and repeat.

Tracks 1–14

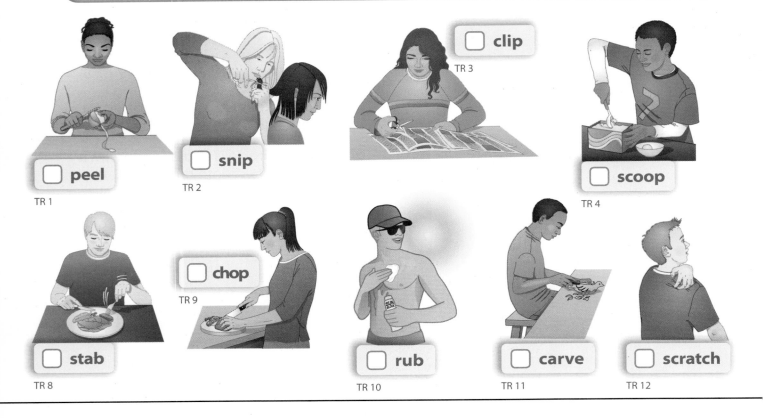

☐ **peel** TR 1

☐ **snip** TR 2

☐ **clip** TR 3

☐ **scoop** TR 4

☐ **stab** TR 8

☐ **chop** TR 9

☐ **rub** TR 10

☐ **carve** TR 11

☐ **scratch** TR 12

Check Your Understanding

A. Underline the correct word to complete each sentence.

1. Sally needs to (**snip** / **stab**) the tags from her shirt.

2. I went into the kitchen to help (**mow** / **slice**) bread for sandwiches.

3. Dad uses a small razor to (**rub** / **shave**) his face.

4. The waiter brought him a knife so that he could (**clip** / **cut**) his steak.

5. To make mashed potatoes, first you must (**peel** / **mow**) the potatoes.

6. Bob (**chopped** / **rubbed**) the meat into little pieces to add to the stew.

7. Luisa likes to (**carve** / **clip**) coupons from the newspaper.

8. Shawn could not stop (**stabbing** / **scratching**) the rash on his arms and legs.

9. When a nurse takes blood, she (**stabs** / **scoops**) your finger with a needle.

10. It is a perfect day to (**carve** / **mow**) the lawn.

11. If you have dry skin, (**dig** / **rub**) some of this lotion on your hands.

cut
TR 5

slice
TR 6

dig
TR 7

mow
TR 13

shave
TR 14

Definitions

If you **carve** an object, you cut it out of wood or stone.

If you **chop** something, you cut it into small pieces with a knife.

When you **clip** something, you cut it with quick, short strokes.

If you **cut** something, you use something sharp to remove part of it or to break it.

If people or animals **dig**, they make a hole in the ground.

If you **mow** an area of grass, you cut it using a machine (called a lawnmower).

When you **peel** fruits or vegetables, you remove their skins.

If you **rub** something, you move a cloth or your fingers backward and forward over it.

If you **scoop** something from a container, you remove it with your hand or with a spoon.

If you **scratch** part of your body, you rub your fingernails against your skin.

If you **shave**, you remove hair from your face or body by cutting it off using a special knife or electric tool.

If you **slice** food, you cut it into thin pieces.

If you **snip** something, you cut it quickly using sharp scissors.

If you **stab** something, you push a knife or a sharp object into it.

12. The wooden chair was (**carved / snipped**) by hand, with great care.

13. To build the highway, the workers had to (**chop / dig**) into the hillside.

14. Could you please (**peel / scoop**) the ice cream into a bowl?

B. Circle the correct answer.

1. Why would you cut your food?

   a. to eat it more easily   b. to make it taste better   c. *a* and *b*

2. Which of the following would you rub on your skin?

   a. ice cream   b. shaving cream   c. sour cream

3. Which of the following might have been carved?

    a. a wooden chair   b. a book   c. *a* and *b*

4. Which of the following might you chop?

    a. an onion   b. a carrot   c. *a* and *b*

5. Which of the following might you clip?

    a. your homework   b. a newspaper article   c. an Internet article

6. Why would you dig?

    a. to pass your science test   b. to find a place to sit   c. to plant flowers

7. Which of the following would you mow?

    a. your grass   b. your carpet   c. *a* and *b*

8. Which of the following would you peel?

    a. a strawberry   b. an orange   c. *a* and *b*

9. Which of the following would you scoop?

    a. a steak   b. a hamburger   c. mashed potatoes

10. Which of the following are you most likely to scratch?

    a. your head   b. your money   c. your lunch

11. Why might a man shave?

    a. because he does not   b. because he has   c. *a* and *b*
       want a beard   hair on his face

12. Which of the following would you slice?

    a. a car   b. an apple   c. a sofa

13. Which of the following would you snip?

    a. a string hanging   b. a long piece of hair   c. *a* and *b*
       from your shirt   that is in front of your eyes

14. Why would somebody stab another person?

    a. to help him   b. to harm him   c. *a* and *b*

Challenge Words

Check (✔) the words you already know.

☐ bulldoze   ☐ grate   ☐ hack   ☐ pierce   ☐ shred

☐ crop   ☐ grind   ☐ mince   ☐ scrape   ☐ slit

254. Weapons and Explosives

Check (✔) the words you already know. Then, listen and repeat.

Tracks 1–7

☐ **arrow**
TR 1

☐ **bomb**
TR 2

☐ **sword**
TR 3

Definitions

An **arrow** is a long, thin weapon that is sharp and pointed at one end.

A **bomb** is a weapon that explodes and damages things nearby.

A **bullet** is a small piece of metal that is shot out of a gun.

A **firecracker** is an object that explodes and makes a loud noise when you light it.

Fireworks are things that shoot up into the air and explode, making bright colors in the sky.

A **gun** is a weapon that shoots bullets.

A **sword** is a weapon with a handle and a long, sharp blade.

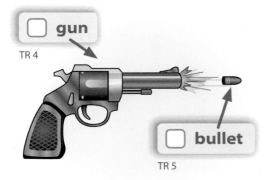

☐ **gun**
TR 4

☐ **bullet**
TR 5

☐ **firecracker**
TR 6

☐ **fireworks**
TR 7

Check Your Understanding

A. Choose the sentence that correctly uses the underlined word.

1. a. The hunter bought <u>bullets</u> for his gun.

   b. The dancer bought <u>bullets</u> for her feet.

2. a. Many years ago, knights carried <u>swords</u>.

   b. Nowadays, it is common for robbers to carry <u>swords</u>.

3. a. After the <u>bomb</u> went off, everybody was calm.

   b. After the <u>bomb</u> went off, everybody ran.

4. a. The loud sound of the <u>firecracker</u> scared the dog.

   b. The <u>firecracker</u> didn't make any noise at all.

5. a. A <u>gun</u> is a weapon that shoots arrows.

   b. A <u>gun</u> is a dangerous weapon.

6. a. The town will have <u>fireworks</u> inside the town hall.

   b. The town will have <u>fireworks</u> to celebrate its 200th anniversary.

7. a. The end of an <u>arrow</u> is sharp and pointed.

   b. The end of an <u>arrow</u> is soft and round.

B. Write **T** for **true statements** and **F** for **false statements**.

1. _____ You can use an arrow to hunt.

2. _____ You would not be able to tell if a bomb went off nearby.

3. _____ You put bullets into your knife to make it fire.

4. _____ Firecrackers make a lot of noise.

5. _____ When a town puts on a fireworks display, people can see bright colors in the sky.

6. _____ A gun is made of metal and uses bullets.

7. _____ These days, it is common to see people fighting with swords.

Challenge Words

Check (✔) the words you already know.

☐ ammunition ☐ boomerang ☐ cannon ☐ dynamite ☐ pistol

☐ arms ☐ bow ☐ dart ☐ firearms ☐ shotgun

275. Engines

Check (✔) the words you already know. Then, listen and repeat.

Tracks 1–5

☐ **engine**
TR 1

Definitions

A **battery** is a small object that provides electricity for things such as radios.

A **brake** is the part in a vehicle that makes it go slower or stop.

The **engine** of a car is the part that produces the power to make the car move.

A **jet** is an aircraft that is powered by jet engines.

A **motor** is a machine that makes something move or work.

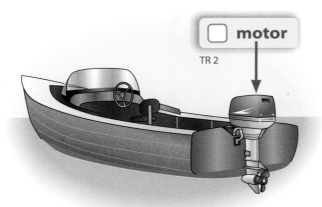

☐ **motor**
TR 2

☐ **battery**
TR 3

☐ **brake**
TR 4

☐ **jet**
TR 5

Check Your Understanding

A. Choose the correct word from the word bank to complete each sentence.

battery	brake	engine	jets	motor

1. It is important that you step on the _____ when you get to a stop sign.

2. At the air show, several _____ did tricks overhead and flew by very fast.

3. Hugo said that he wanted to call last night, but the _____ in his cell phone was dead.

4. Does your boat have a _____, or do you have to row it?

5. The race car has a large _____ that allows it to move very fast.

B. Circle the item that is most needed in each situation.

1. I am in New York, but I need to be in Los Angeles later today.

   a. battery　　　　　　b. jet　　　　　　c. brake

2. My watch has stopped running.

   a. brake　　　　　　b. engine　　　　　　c. battery

3. I am in a hurry and want my car to go fast.

   a. brake　　　　　　b. jet　　　　　　c. engine

4. Our boat is not moving.

   a. motor　　　　　　b. jet　　　　　　c. brake

5. The traffic light is about to turn red.

   a. motor　　　　　　b. battery　　　　　　c. brake

Challenge Words

Check (✔) the words you already know.

☐ crankshaft　　　☐ headset　　　☐ starter　　　☐ turbine

☐ gear　　　☐ piston　　　☐ throttle

276. Electronics

Check (✔) the words you already know. Then, listen and repeat.

 Tracks 1–5

☐ **robot**
TR 1

Definitions

A **computer** is an electronic machine that can store and handle large amounts of information.

The **keyboard** of a computer is the set of keys that you press in order to operate it.

A **monitor** is a screen that shows information from the computer.

A **mouse** is an object that you use to do things on a computer without using the keyboard.

A **robot** is a machine that can move and perform tasks that people might do.

☐ **computer**
TR 2

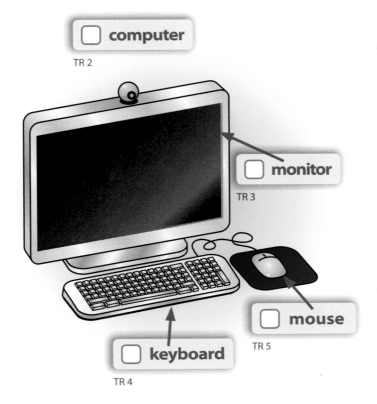

☐ **monitor**
TR 3

☐ **mouse**
TR 5

☐ **keyboard**
TR 4

Check Your Understanding

A. Match each word to the correct description. One description will not be used.

1. _____ computer
2. _____ keyboard
3. _____ monitor
4. _____ mouse
5. _____ robot

a. a type of machine or computer; does jobs that people might do

b. a small device that you move with your hand to control a computer

c. a device that controls heating or cooling

d. a machine on which you can create, get, and store information

e. a flat object covered with keys that controls the computer

f. a screen where information from your computer is displayed

B. Underline the correct word to complete each sentence.

1. I took my (**computer / robot**) on the plane so that I could get some work done.

2. My dad wishes he had a (**monitor / robot**) to clean the house for him.

3. Move your (**mouse / keyboard**) to click on that icon.

4. You cannot see any information because your (**keyboard / monitor**) is not turned on.

5. The letters on my (**robot / keyboard**) stick, so I often make mistakes when I type.

Challenge Words

Check (✔) the words you already know.

☐ bit   ☐ format   ☐ network   ☐ register   ☐ thermostat

☐ chip   ☐ memory   ☐ projector   ☐ terminal   ☐ transistor

314. Lubricants and Fuels

Check (✔) the words you already know. Then, listen and repeat.

Tracks 1–4

☐ **oil**

TR 1

Definitions

Fuel is a substance such as coal or oil that is burned to provide heat or power.

Gas is a liquid that you put into a car or other vehicle to make it work. *Gas* is short for *gasoline*.

Grease is a thick substance similar to oil that helps make parts of a machine work better.

Oil is a smooth, thick liquid that is used for making machines run. Oil is found underground.

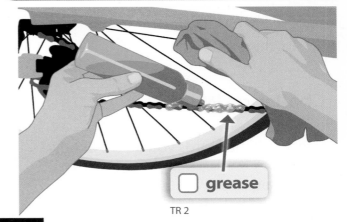

☐ **grease**

TR 2

☐ **fuel**

TR 3

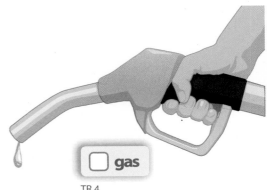

☐ **gas**

TR 4

Check Your Understanding

A. Write **T** for **true statements** and **F** for **false statements**.

1. _____ Coal is a type of fuel.

2. _____ Gas is found under the ground.

3. _____ Putting grease on machine parts will make them run more smoothly.

4. _____ Oil will cause a machine to stop running.

B. Circle the correct answer to complete each sentence.

1. You may need fuel in order to _____.

   a. take a nap   b. heat your house   c. *a* and *b*

2. If you do not have gas in your car, _____.

   a. it will go very slowly   b. it will go very fast   c. it will not go

3. You might get grease on your hands when you _____.

   a. repair your car   b. drive your car   c. clean your car

4. Oil comes from _____.

   a. the water   b. underground   c. your car

Challenge Words

Check (✔) the words you already know.

☐ diesel   ☐ lubrication   ☐ refuel

☐ lubricate   ☐ petroleum   ☐ turpentine

315. Handles

Check (✔) the words you already know. Then, listen and repeat.

Tracks 1–3

Definitions

A **doorknob** is a round handle on a door.

A **handle** is an object that is attached to a door or a drawer, and is used for opening and closing.

A **knob** is a round handle or switch.

audio

☐ **knob**

TR 1

☐ **doorknob**

TR 2

☐ **handle**

TR 3

Check Your Understanding

A. Underline the correct word to complete each sentence.

1. Turn the (**doorknob / handle**) to open the door.

2. Turn the (**knob / doorknob**) to play the music louder.

3. Pull the (**doorknob / handle**) to open the drawer.

B. Circle the correct answer.

1. You use a doorknob to _____ .

    a. open a door   b. look through a door   c. *a* and *b*

2. You use a handle to _____ .

    a. open a drawer   b. close a drawer   c. *a* and *b*

3. You use a knob to _____ .

    a. turn up the volume   b. find the right station   c. *a* and *b*

Challenge Words

Check (✔) the words you already know.

☐ grip   ☐ hilt

316. Miscellaneous Devices

Check (✔) the words you already know. Then, listen and repeat.

Tracks 1–5

☐ **dial**

TR 1

Definitions

A **dial** is a small knob on a machine that you can move in order to control the way the machine works.

A **ladder** is a device used for reaching high places. It is made of short steps that are between two long pieces of wood or metal.

A **pedal** in a car or on a machine is a part that you press with your foot in order to control the machine.

A **switch** is a small control for turning electricity on or off.

The **trigger** of a gun is the part that you pull to make it shoot.

☐ **trigger**

TR 2

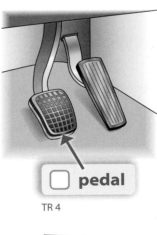

☐ **pedal**

TR 4

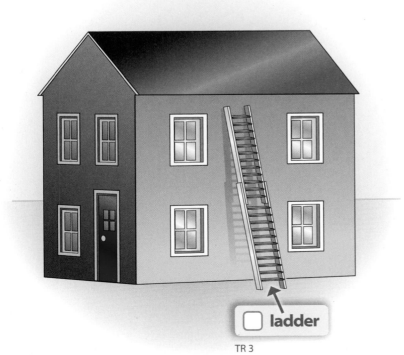

☐ **ladder**

TR 3

☐ **switch**

TR 5

Check Your Understanding

A. Unscramble the letters to make a word. Then, match each word to the correct description.

	Word	Description	
1. rgtireg	_____	_____	a. something that you push up to make the lights come on
2. twicsh	_____	_____	b. something that you pull to fire a water pistol
3. lida	_____	_____	c. something that you use to reach high places
4. delpa	_____	_____	d. something that you push with your feet to control certain machines
5. dralde	_____	_____	e. something that you turn with your hand to control certain machines

B. Underline the correct word to complete each sentence.

1. The man climbed the (**dial / ladder**) to reach the windows on the second floor.

2. As soon as he pulled the (**trigger / pedal**), Paul knew that he had missed the target.

3. To start the washing machine, just put soap in and turn the (**ladder / dial**).

4. The pianist played the keys with his hands and the (**triggers / pedals**) with his feet to make wonderful sounds.

5. This (**switch / trigger**) turns on the lights in the kitchen.

Challenge Words

Check (✔) the words you already know.

☐ barometer ☐ crank ☐ platform ☐ pulley
☐ baton ☐ easel ☐ pointer

419. Machines

Check (✔) the word if you already know it. Then, listen and repeat.

 Track 1

☐ **machine**

TR 1

Definition

A **machine** is a piece of equipment that uses electricity or an engine to do a particular job.

Check Your Understanding

A. Check (✔) each activity in the list that might be easier if you used a machine.

☐ drinking a cup of coffee

☐ making a cup of coffee

☐ wearing a new shirt

☐ sewing a new shirt

☐ washing the dishes

☐ eating dinner

B. Write **T** for **true statements** and **F** for **false statements**.

1. _____ Machines are only found in factories, not in homes.

2. _____ A car is a type of machine.

3. _____ There are machines in your school that help both students and teachers do their work.

Challenge Words

Check (✔) the words you already know.

☐ apparatus ☐ clockwork ☐ equipment ☐ hardware ☐ mechanical

☐ appliance ☐ contraption ☐ gadget ☐ machinery ☐ rig

420. Vision-Related Equipment

Check (✔) the word if you already know it. Then, listen and repeat.

 Track 1

☐ **camera**

TR 1

Definition

A **camera** is a piece of equipment for taking photographs or making movies.

Check Your Understanding

A. Circle the correct answer.

1. What does a camera look like?

   a. It might be small and rectangular, with buttons on it.

   b. It might be very large and ball-like, with buttons on it.

2. What does a camera do?

   a. It takes photos for you to print later.

   b. It prints photos but does not take them.

3. When might you use a camera?

   a. You would use a camera when you are brushing your teeth.

   b. You would use a camera when you go on vacation.

B. Write **T** for **true statements** and **F** for **false statements**.

1. _____ Cameras are very difficult to find, and few people have them.

2. _____ You might bring a camera to your graduation from school.

3. _____ Cameras are used only for watching movies.

4. _____ Some cameras will record movies for you to watch later.

Challenge Words

Check (✔) the words you already know.

☐ binoculars   ☐ eyepiece   ☐ lens   ☐ microscope   ☐ telescope

143. Board / Other Games

Check (✔) the words you already know. Then, listen and repeat.

 Tracks 1–5

☐ **doll**
TR 1

Definitions

A **doll** is a child's toy that looks like a small person or baby.

A **puppet** is a small model of a person or animal that you can move by putting your hand inside of it.

A **puzzle** is a question or a game that is difficult to answer correctly or to put together properly.

A **toy** is an object that children play with.

Toys are objects that children play with.

☐ **puppet**
TR 2

☐ **puzzle**
TR 3

☐ **toys**
TR 4

☐ **toy**
TR 5

Check Your Understanding

A. Unscramble the letters to make a word. Then, match each word with the correct description.

	Word	Description

1. yost _____ _____ a. an item that a child plays with

2. pteupp _____ _____ b. a small toy that looks like a baby or a little person

3. uzelzp _____ _____ c. something that you need to use your mind to figure out

4. lold _____ _____

5. oyt _____ _____ d. a small model animal that you move with your hands

e. more than one toy

B. Underline the correct word to complete each sentence.

1. Jimmy accidentally stepped on his (**toy / toys**) and broke them.

2. When I was a little girl, I would dress my (**dolls / puzzles**) up and play with them.

3. Today in school, we did a (**puzzle / toy**) called a "word search."

4. I think that Maggie's new blocks have become her favorite (**toy / puppet**).

5. One of my favorite TV shows uses (**puppets / toys**) to act out the story, instead of real people.

Challenge Words

Check (✔) the words you already know.

☐ cards ☐ chess ☐ dice ☐ marionette ☐ raffle

☐ checkers ☐ crossword ☐ hopscotch ☐ pinball

158. Recreation / Sports Equipment

Check (✔) the words you already know. Then, listen and repeat.

 Tracks 1–9

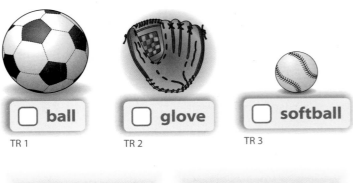

- ☐ **ball**
  TR 1
- ☐ **glove**
  TR 2
- ☐ **softball**
  TR 3

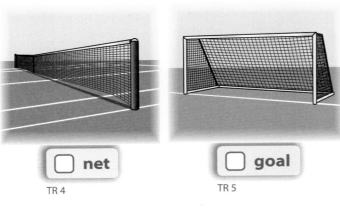

- ☐ **net**
  TR 4
- ☐ **goal**
  TR 5

- ☐ **touchdown**
  TR 6
- ☐ **bat**
  TR 7

Definitions

A **ball** is a round object that is used in games such as tennis and soccer.

A **base** is one of four squares on a baseball field that runners step on when they try to score.

A **bat** is a long piece of wood or metal that is used for hitting the ball in games such as baseball.

A **glove** is a covering for the hand that you might wear to play certain sports, such as baseball or boxing.

In games such as soccer, the **goal** is the place where the players try to get the ball in order to score a point for their team.

In sports such as tennis, the **net** is the object that you hit the ball over.

A **softball** is similar to a baseball, but it is larger.

To **swing** means to try to hit something by moving your arms forward and backward in a half circle.

A **touchdown** is the act of scoring points in U.S. football by taking the ball over the goal line.

- ☐ **swing**
  TR 8

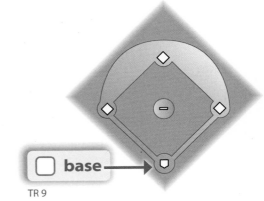

- ☐ **base**
  TR 9

Check Your Understanding

A. Circle the word in each group that does not belong with the **boldfaced** word on the left.

1. **ball**	football	soccer	hockey
2. **bat**	swing	touchdown	softball
3. **glove**	boxing	baseball	net
4. **swing**	football	baseball	golf
5. **base**	softball	baseball	golf
6. **goal**	hockey	soccer	softball
7. **net**	volleyball	swimming	tennis
8. **softball**	base	bat	goal
9. **touchdown**	football	bat	goal

B. Write **T** for **true statements** and **F** for **false statements**.

1. _____ You need a ball to play tennis.

2. _____ A bat is a long piece of plastic.

3. _____ Baseball players wear a glove to help them catch the ball.

4. _____ If you swing at a ball, you try to hit it.

5. _____ A softball is a lot like a basketball.

6. _____ The goal is the area a team must protect so that the other team does not score a point.

7. _____ A baseball player must throw the bases to score a point.

8. _____ A net is needed for games such as tennis.

9. _____ When a hockey player scores, he yells, "Touchdown!"

Challenge Words

Check (✔) the words you already know.

☐ arcade	☐ defense	☐ inning	☐ offense	☐ puck
☐ carousel	☐ homer	☐ knockout	☐ out	☐ target

183. Recreation and Sports

Check (✔) the words you already know. Then, listen and repeat.

 Tracks 1–6

☐ **game**

TR 1

☐ **recess**

TR 2

Definitions

A **contest** is a competition or a game where there is a winner.

A **game** is an activity or a sport in which you try to win against someone.

A **race** is a competition to see who is the fastest.

In a school, **recess** is the period of time when students are allowed to play.

Recreation is an activity that you do in your free time to relax.

A **sport** is a game or other activity that requires physical effort and skill.

☐ **contest**

TR 3

☐ **recreation**

TR 4

☐ **race**

TR 5

☐ **sport**

TR 6

107

Check Your Understanding

A. Complete the paragraph with the correct word from the word bank. Use each word only once.

game	races	sport
recess	contest	recreation

My favorite part of the school day is (1) _____. Once I am out in the

schoolyard, my friends and I do many different things. We often play a (2) _____,

especially baseball. Other times, we do something else for (3) _____, such

as playing on the playground. We might have relay (4) _____ to see who

is the fastest runner. We might also have a (5) _____ to see who can jump the

farthest. When it rains, and we cannot go outside, our teacher lets us play an indoor

(6) _____ such as checkers.

B. Choose the sentence that correctly uses the underlined word.

1. a. I have so many <u>games</u>, I cannot stop sleeping.

   b. I love to play <u>games</u>, especially chess.

2. a. We took our test during <u>recess</u>.

   b. We played in the schoolyard during <u>recess</u>.

3. a. Annie entered her painting into the school's art <u>contest</u>.

   b. Annie packed her lunch for the art <u>contest</u>.

4. a. Peter won the <u>race</u> by running a mile in under five minutes.

   b. Peter won the <u>race</u> by studying in the library.

5. a. Weekends are for rest and <u>recreation</u>.

   b. Weekdays are for hard work and <u>recreation</u>.

6. a. Eric's favorite <u>sport</u> is sleeping.

   b. Eric's favorite <u>sport</u> is hockey.

Challenge Words

Check (✔) the words you already know.

☐ compete   ☐ derby   ☐ marathon   ☐ tournament

☐ competition   ☐ hobby   ☐ match

209. Sports (Specific Types)

Check (✔) the words you already know. Then, listen and repeat.

Tracks 1–20

☐ **baseball**
TR 1

☐ **golf**
TR 2

☐ **bicycle**
TR 3

☐ **bowling**
TR 4

☐ **racing**
TR 5

☐ **skate**
TR 7

☐ **football**
TR 6

☐ **skating**
TR 8

☐ **basketball**
TR 9

☐ **hockey**
TR 10

☐ **boxing**
TR 11

Definitions

Baseball is a game that is played with a bat and a ball on a large field by two teams of nine players. Players must hit the ball and run around four bases to score.

Basketball is a game in which two teams of five players each try to throw a large ball through a round net hanging from a high metal ring.

A **bicycle** is a vehicle with two wheels. You ride it by sitting on it and using your feet to make the wheels turn.

Bowling is a game in which you roll a heavy ball down a narrow track toward a group of wooden objects called pins and try to knock them down.

Boxing is a sport in which two people fight following special rules.

Football is a game for two teams of eleven players. Each team tries to win points by kicking, carrying, or throwing the ball into an area at the other end of the field called the end zone.

Golf is a game where you use long metal clubs to hit a small, hard ball into holes.

Hockey is a game that is played on ice between two teams who try to score goals. Players use long, curved sticks to hit a small rubber disk called a puck.

Racing is the sport of competing in races such as car or horse races.

When you **skate**, you move around a surface wearing skates.

Skating is the act of moving around on ice or the ground while wearing shoes with blades or wheels.

(Continued)

skiing
TR 12

swimming
TR 13

swim
TR 15

ski
TR 14

soccer
TR 16

wrestling
TR 17

volleyball
TR 18

tennis
TR 20

softball
TR 19

Definitions

When you **ski**, you move over snow or water on skis.

Skiing is the sport of sliding down or across snowy surfaces on skis.

Soccer is a game played by two teams of eleven players using a round ball. Players kick the ball to each other and try to score goals by kicking the ball into a large net. Outside the United States, this game is also called **football.**

Softball is a game similar to baseball, but it is played with a larger, softer ball.

When you **swim,** you move through water by making movements with your arms and legs.

Swimming is the act of moving through the water, especially as a sport or for pleasure.

Tennis is a game for two or four players, who use rackets to hit a ball across a net between them.

Volleyball is a game in which two teams hit a large ball over a high net with their arms or hands.

Wrestling is the sport in which people fight each other by trying to throw their opponent to the ground.

Check Your Understanding

A. Circle the correct answer to each question.

1. Which of these do you need to play baseball?

   a. a racket   b. a pool   c. a bat

2. What is soccer called outside of the United States?

   a. softball   b. football   c. volleyball

3. How is softball different from baseball?

   a. The bat is larger.   b. The ball is larger.   c. The team is smaller.

4. What activity allows you to move through water?

   a. skiing   b. skating   c. swimming

5. Basketball can be played in which place?

    a. outdoors   b. on ice   c. in the water

6. If you are using a big ball to knock down pins, what are you doing?

    a. playing basketball   b. playing baseball   c. bowling

7. In what sport do people fight while following special rules?

    a. tennis   b. boxing   c. swimming

8. What is the goal of a game of football?

    a. put the ball in the end zone   b. put the ball in the basket   c. put the ball in a cup

9. In golf, which type of equipment do you use?

    a. a bat and ball   b. a glove and mask   c. a set of metal clubs

10. The game of hockey is played on what kind of surface?

    a. grass   b. wood   c. ice

11. Which might you watch in racing?

    a. balls   b. cars   c. cats

12. In what season would you probably skate outside?

    a. fall   b. spring   c. winter

13. Where might you go skiing?

    a. on a mountain   b. in a stream   c. on a court

14. Which equipment would you use to play tennis?

    a. a puck, skates, and a stick   b. a racquet, ball, and a net   c. a ball, glove, and a bat

15. What do you need to play volleyball?

    a. a net and a ball   b. gloves   c. a set of metal clubs

16. For which sport would you need mats on the ground to prevent injury?

    a. hockey   b. wrestling   c. swimming

17. Where can you swim?

    a. in school or at home   b. in a pool or the ocean   c. in a park or a field

18. What do you need in order to go skating?

    a. special shoes with wheels or blades

    b. special red shoes

    c. no shoes

19. How many wheels does a bicycle have?

    a. one

    b. two

    c. four

20. Where might you ski?

    a. on the water   b. on the side of a mountain   c. both *a* and *b*

B. Choose the correct word from the word bank to complete each sentence.

skiing	golf	soccer	skate	bicycle
wrestling	hockey	baseball	swimming	basketball

1. It feels so good to jump in the water and go _____ on a hot day.

2. With all the snow outside, it makes me want to go _____ .

3. Today, Jim and I are going to play _____ , and I will share my clubs with him.

4. Matt likes to ride his _____ to school.

5. My grandfather gave me the bat he used when he played _____ in high school.

6. If you want to play _____ , you need to be able to kick the ball while you run.

7. The player stopped the puck, and his team became the _____ champions.

8. Nick won the _____ match when he threw his opponent to the ground.

9. The _____ player scored three points when the ball went into the basket.

10. I cannot _____ backwards like that. I would fall on the ice if I tried.

swim	racing	boxing	ski	tennis
softball	bowling	football	skating	volleyball

11. The people were playing _____ at the net on the beach.

12. My mother just got a new _____ racket for her birthday.

13. I can only _____ down the very small hills, and I go very slowly.

14. I get so excited when my favorite _____ team scores a touchdown.

15. Mary wanted to be the pitcher for her school's _____ team.

16. _____ can be tricky because moving on ice without falling is not easy.

17. Most people wear gloves when they are _____ .

18. My daughter loves to _____ in the ocean.

19. Car _____ might be fun to watch, but I do not like it when they crash.

20. My little brother is too small to go _____ . He won't be able to lift that heavy ball.

Challenge Words

Check (✔) the words you already know.

☐ archery   ☐ badminton   ☐ croquet   ☐ fencing   ☐ lacrosse

304. Exercise

Check (✔) the words you already know. Then, listen and repeat.

Tracks 1–3

☐ **exercise**

TR 1

Definitions

To **exercise** means to move your body in order to stay healthy and strong.

To **practice** means to do something regularly in order to get better at it.

To **stretch** means to put your arms or legs out very straight, often right before or after you exercise.

☐ **practice**

TR 2

☐ **stretch**

TR 3

Check Your Understanding

A. Circle the correct answer.

1. Why should you exercise?

   a. to earn a lot of money

   b. to get good grades

   c. to be healthy

2. How do you practice something?

   a. You do it one time.

   b. You think about doing it.

   c. You do it over and over again.

3. When is it most important for you to stretch?

   a. while you are eating

   b. before and after you exercise

   c. while you are giving your dog a bath

B. Underline the correct word to complete each sentence.

1. Tim (**practices / exercises**) soccer every day after school.

2. Wendy (**stretches / exercises**) by running two miles every day.

3. Rochelle (**stretches / practices**) her whole body out during her yoga class.

Challenge Words

Check (✔) the words you already know.

☐ cartwheel   ☐ somersault   ☐ workout

☐ jog   ☐ sprint   ☐ yoga

370. Magic

Check (✔) the words you already know. Then, listen and repeat.

Tracks 1–2

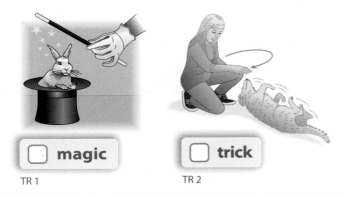

☐ magic

TR 1

☐ trick

TR 2

Definitions

Magic is the use of tricks, performed by a person, in order to entertain people.

A **trick** is a clever action that someone or something does to entertain or confuse others.

Check Your Understanding

A. Circle the correct answer.

1. Which is the best example of magic?

   a. making a bird appear out of nowhere

   b. explaining how birds fly south in the winter

   c. holding a bird and then letting it fly away

2. Which is the best example of a trick?

   a. building a house made of cards with your mother

   b. having your mother deal the cards so that you can play a card game

   c. having your mother pick a card, and then telling her which one she has

3. Which of the items below is <u>not</u> a trick?

   a. making a cake

   b. making a lady disappear

   c. making a coin appear behind your ear

B. Write **T** for **true statements** and **F** for **false statements**.

1. _____ The purpose of magic is to bore people.

2. _____ It is always easy to figure out how a trick is done.

3. _____ Magic is often done during special shows.

4. _____ A trick usually entertains or confuses people.

Challenge Words

Check (✔) the words you already know.

☐ gimmick   ☐ stunt

107. Building and Repairing

Check (✔) the words you already know. Then, listen and repeat.

Tracks 1–9

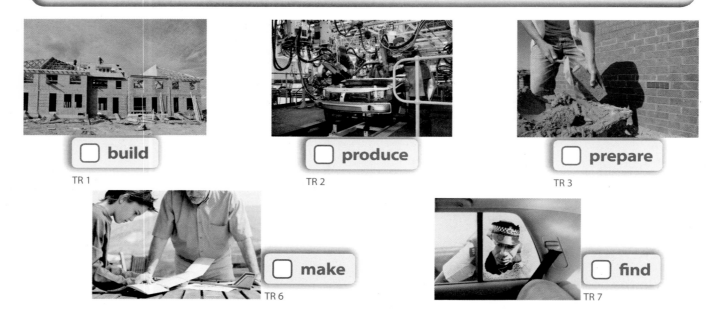

☐ build
TR 1

☐ produce
TR 2

☐ prepare
TR 3

☐ make
TR 6

☐ find
TR 7

Check Your Understanding

A. Choose the correct word from the word bank to complete each sentence.

fix	shape	making
find	repairs	produce
build	prepare	developed

1. I need a hammer so that I can _____ my broken bicycle.

2. They are planning to _____ a new arena in town.

3. The librarian looked, but she could not _____ the book that I asked her for.

4. In this factory, they _____ cars and other vehicles.

5. Robbie is _____ a new table and chairs from scrap wood.

6. After years of practice, Sarah has _____ into a talented musician.

7. John _____ people's refrigerators when they break.

8. We will _____ this clay into flowerpots.

9. What should we do to _____ for the big test next week?

Definitions

To **build** means to make something by joining things together.

To **develop** means to grow or change over a period of time.

To **find** means to see something after you have been looking for it.

To **fix** something means to repair it.

To **make** something means to produce, build, or create it.

To **prepare** means to make something ready.

To **produce** means to make or grow something.

To **repair** means to fix something that has been damaged or is not working properly.

To **shape** means to use your hands or other tools to give something a particular shape.

☐ repair
TR 4

☐ develop
TR 5

☐ fix
TR 8

☐ shape
TR 9

B. Underline the correct word to complete each sentence.

1. William (**prepares / produces**) for his exams by taking practice tests.

2. Sally (**shaped / built**) the cookie dough into little stars before she put them into the oven.

3. Is the person who (**repairs / finds**) your car a good mechanic?

4. Let's both try to (**find / make**) my keys, or we won't be able to leave.

5. Rose's simple idea (**made / developed**) into this wonderful restaurant.

6. Many of the things we use every day are (**shaped / produced**) in other countries.

7. Does anybody know how to (**build / fix**) this old broken TV?

8. Annie (**made / built**) jewelry to sell for extra money.

9. How long ago did they (**develop / build**) your house?

Challenge Words

Check (✔) the words you already know.

☐ construct   ☐ establish   ☐ generate   ☐ manufacture   ☐ preserve

☐ create   ☐ form   ☐ install   ☐ modify   ☐ process

117

164. Containers

Check (✔) the words you already know. Then, listen and repeat.

 Tracks 1–21

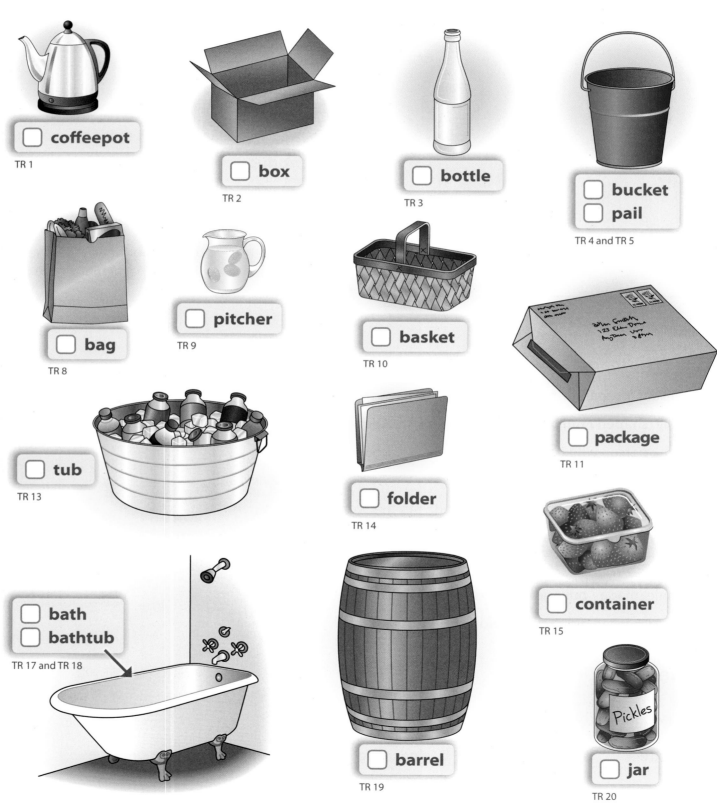

☐ **coffeepot**
TR 1

☐ **box**
TR 2

☐ **bottle**
TR 3

☐ **bucket**
☐ **pail**
TR 4 and TR 5

☐ **bag**
TR 8

☐ **pitcher**
TR 9

☐ **basket**
TR 10

☐ **package**
TR 11

☐ **tub**
TR 13

☐ **folder**
TR 14

☐ **container**
TR 15

☐ **bath**
☐ **bathtub**
TR 17 and TR 18

☐ **barrel**
TR 19

☐ **jar**
TR 20

jug
TR 6

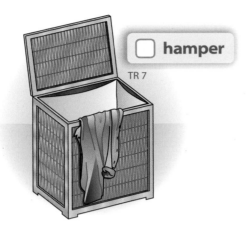

hamper
TR 7

suitcase
TR 12

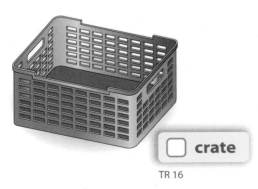

crate
TR 16

sack
TR 21

Definitions

A **bag** is a container made of paper, plastic, or leather, and is used for carrying things.

A **barrel** is a large container with curved sides and flat ends that is usually used for storing liquids.

A **basket** is a container made from thin strips of wood, plastic, or metal, and is used for carrying or storing objects.

A **bath** or a **bathtub** is a long container that you fill with water and sit or lie in to wash your body.

A **bottle** is a glass or plastic container in which drinks and other liquids are kept.

A **box** is a container with a hard bottom, hard sides, and usually a lid.

A **bucket** is a round metal or plastic container with a handle. **Buckets** are often used for holding and carrying water.

A **coffeepot** is a pot used for making and serving coffee.

A **container** is a box that is used for holding or storing things.

A **crate** is a large box used for moving or storing things.

A **folder** is a folded piece of cardboard or plastic that you keep papers in.

A **hamper** is a large container with a cover that holds dirty clothes until they are washed.

A **jar** is a glass container with a lid that is used for storing food.

A **jug** is a container with a handle used for holding and pouring liquids.

A **package** is something wrapped in paper, in a box, or in an envelope.

A **pail** is a round metal or plastic container with a handle. **Pails** are often used for holding and carrying items, such as sand.

A **pitcher** is a tall, round container with an open top and a large handle that is used for holding and pouring liquids.

A **sack** is a large bag made of thick paper or rough material.

A **suitcase** is a case for carrying your clothes when you travel.

A **tub** is a deep container of any size.

Check Your Understanding

A. Write **T** for **true statements** and **F** for **false statements**.

1. _____ You might give your dog a bath in a bathtub.

2. _____ You pack your suitcase every day to go to school.

3. _____ A barrel is a small plastic container where you might keep books or folders.

4. _____ A hamper is used to store your clean clothes until it is time to wear them.

5. _____ In a restaurant, you might see a basket of bread on your table.

6. _____ A sack is only ever made of plastic or metal.

7. _____ Pickles and peanut butter are two foods that come in jars.

8. _____ You use a folder to carry heavy things.

9. _____ Coffeepots are used to make and serve coffee.

10. _____ If you want to take your cat on an airplane, you need to put her in a crate.

11. _____ You might keep food in containers in your refrigerator.

12. _____ When you go shopping, you carry the things you buy in a jug.

13. _____ You can use a pail to carry water.

14. _____ You might receive a package in the mail.

15. _____ Glass is the only material used to make bottles.

16. _____ Most people carry their groceries home in bags.

17. _____ You might serve water or juice in a pitcher.

18. _____ A bucket is something that you drink from.

19. _____ You use a tub to make and serve coffee.

20. _____ People put their things into boxes when they move to a new home.

21. _____ You usually stand up to take a bath.

B. Underline the correct word to complete each sentence.

1. There is a (**jug** / **folder**) of apple cider on the table.

2. Olivia, please carry your (**bathtub** / **hamper**) to the washing machine so that I can wash your clothes.

3. It is better for the environment if you bring your own (**tubs** / **bags**) to the grocery store.

4. The (**coffeepot** / **basket**) of flowers sitting on the table looks beautiful.

5. The lid on this (**jar** / **crate**) of salsa is difficult to twist off.

6. George made olive oil and kept it in large, wooden (**barrels / sacks**) until it was time to sell it.

7. Betsy put the (**coffeepot / hamper**) on the tray with cream and sugar.

8. Aunt Mary puts all her craft things into (**pitchers / containers**) and labels them.

9. I wonder what is in the (**suitcase / package**) that arrived in the mail today.

10. After he lost his job, Jim packed his things into a (**pail / box**) and left the office.

11. Matt filled a (**folder / bucket**) with water and went outside to wash his car.

12. Laura prefers to drink water out of a (**bottle / crate**) because she says it tastes better.

13. Please pick up a (**suitcase / sack**) of potatoes for me when you are at the store.

14. The mother gave her children a (**bath / crate**) after they got back from the playground.

15. These (**pitchers / folders**) have students' names on them and have corrected homework inside them.

16. Every time we go to Grandma's house, she serves us a (**pitcher / pail**) of lemonade.

17. This bathroom has a shower on one side, and a (**bucket / bathtub**) on the other side.

18. All our (**barrels / suitcases**) are in the car. We are ready to leave for vacation.

19. There was a hole in the bottom of the old (**folder / tub**), so we couldn't keep water in it.

20. Airplanes have an area where pets can travel, so long as they are in (**jars / crates**).

21. Elsa put all the seashells she found on the beach into her little red (**coffeepot / pail**).

Challenge Words

Check (✔) the words you already know.

- [ ] baggage
- [ ] basin
- [ ] cargo
- [ ] case
- [ ] compartment
- [ ] envelope
- [ ] holder
- [ ] luggage
- [ ] packet
- [ ] shipment

181. Wooden Building Materials

Check (✔) the words you already know. Then, listen and repeat.

 Tracks 1–6

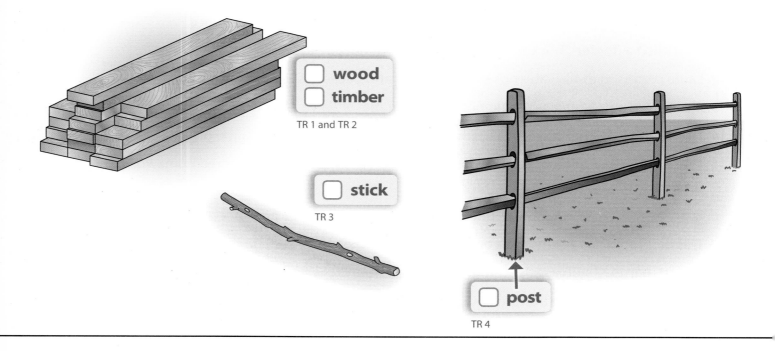

☐ **wood**
☐ **timber**

TR 1 and TR 2

☐ **stick**

TR 3

☐ **post**

TR 4

Check Your Understanding

A. Match each word to the correct definition. One definition will not be used.

1. _____ stick

2. _____ wood

3. _____ board

4. _____ log

5. _____ post

6. _____ timber

a. a piece of wood that has been cut into a thin, rectangular piece

b. a piece of wood or metal that goes into the ground to hold something up

c. an amount of wood used for building or making things

d. a small piece of wood that has broken off of a tree

e. a sheet of material that is made of several layers of wood

f. the large, round part of a cut tree

g. the material that comes from trees

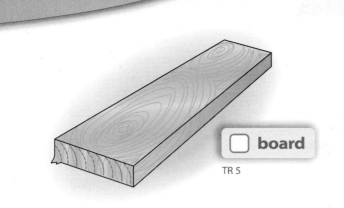

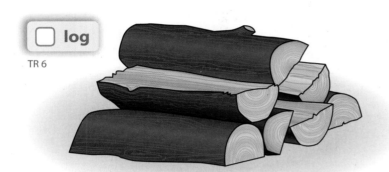

board

TR 5

log

TR 6

Definitions

A **board** is a flat, thin piece of wood.

A **log** is a thick piece of wood that has been cut from a tree.

A **post** is a strong piece of wood or metal that is set into the ground.

A **stick** is a thin branch from a tree.

Timber is wood that is used for building and making things.

Wood is the hard material that trees are made of.

B. Underline the correct word to complete each sentence.

1. Matt was hitting a (**stick / log**) against the ground as he walked.

2. The workers were putting the (**posts / wood**) into the ground to build a fence.

3. The truck was loaded with (**post / timber**) that would be made into a house.

4. We need to find four or five (**logs / boards**) for the campfire.

5. Is that desk made of (**post / wood**) from an oak tree or a cherry tree?

6. The workers laid down flat, wooden (**logs / boards**) as flooring.

Challenge Words

Check (✔) the words you already know.

 lumber

 palette

☐ panel

☐ pillar

☐ plywood

☐ shingle

123

251. Building Materials (General)

Check (✔) the words you already know. Then, listen and repeat.

Tracks 1–9

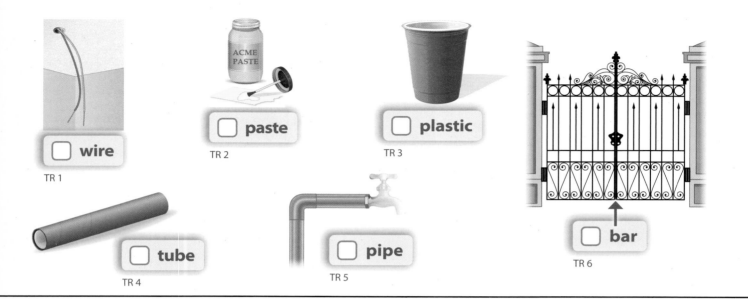

☐ wire
TR 1

☐ paste
TR 2

☐ plastic
TR 3

☐ bar
TR 6

☐ tube
TR 4

☐ pipe
TR 5

Check Your Understanding

A. Write **T** for **true statements** and **F** for **false statements**.

1. _____ Bars are made of plastic and are used to build houses.

2. _____ Bricks are shaped like circles and are very light.

3. _____ Cardboard is often used to make boxes.

4. _____ Builders often use paste to build houses.

5. _____ Water in your home travels through pipes.

6. _____ Bottles are often made of plastic.

7. _____ A sewer system is found above ground.

8. _____ A tube has a square shape and is solid inside.

9. _____ Electronic devices generally have wires.

B. Underline the correct word to complete each sentence.

1. Our hamsters drink their water through a (**bar / tube**).

2. She wants a house made of (**cardboard / brick**).

3. The water travels from the sink drain into the (**sewer / paste**).

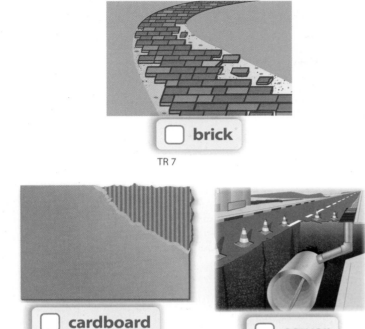

□ brick

TR 7

□ cardboard

TR 8

□ sewer

TR 9

Definitions

A **bar** is a long, straight piece of metal.

A **brick** is a rectangular block used for building walls or paths.

Cardboard is thick, stiff paper that is used for making boxes.

Paste is a thin, wet substance used to stick pieces of paper together.

Plastic is a light but strong material that is produced by a chemical process.

A **pipe** is a long tube through which a liquid or a gas can flow.

A **sewer** is a large pipe under the ground that carries waste and rain water away.

A **tube** is a long, hollow object that is usually round, like a pipe.

A **wire** is a long, thin piece of metal.

4. It is much safer to carry (**pipe / plastic**) bottles because they do not break.

5. After he finished using the (**wire / paste**), Tom had to wash it off of his hands.

6. How do you know which (**brick / wire**) connects the TV to the DVD player?

7. Melanie is afraid of her dog getting out, so she had (**cardboard / bars**) put on her door to keep him in.

8. If your house is too cold in the winter, your (**pipes / bricks**) might freeze.

9. Please put all these books in that (**wire / cardboard**) box.

Challenge Words

Check (✔) the words you already know.

□ cement   □ concrete   □ pavement   □ pole   □ support

□ ceramic   □ fixture   □ plaster   □ putty   □ tile

268. Objects / Materials Used to Cover Things

Check (✔) the words you already know. Then, listen and repeat.

Tracks 1–5

□ mask
TR 1

□ cover
TR 2

Check Your Understanding

A. Choose the correct word from the word bank to complete each sentence.

cork	covers	flap	lid	masks

1. On some holidays, it is common for people to wear _____ to hide who they are.

2. They could not open the bottle because the _____ was stuck inside.

3. You need to put a _____ on that container so that the meat does not dry out.

4. The teacher asked her students to put _____ on all of their books.

5. Fold the _____ over on that envelope so that the paper clips do not fall out.

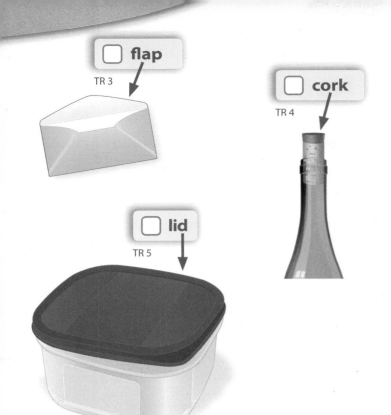

flap
TR 3

cork
TR 4

lid
TR 5

Definitions

A **cork** is an object that you push into the top of a bottle to close it.

A **cover** is something that you put over an object to protect it.

A **flap** is a flat piece of material that is attached to one side of something and can move up, down, or from side to side.

A **lid** is the top of a container that can be removed.

A **mask** is something that you wear over your face to protect it or to hide it.

B. Match each word to the correct definition. One description will not be used.

1. _____ cork
2. _____ cover
3. _____ flap
4. _____ lid
5. _____ mask

a. an item that protects an object

b. what you use to cover a jar or a container

c. a small item that is used to close a bottle

d. something that moves up, down, or side to side

e. clear material used to wrap up food

f. what you wear to hide or protect your face

Challenge Words

Check (✔) the words you already know.

☐ camouflage   ☐ cellophane   ☐ plug   ☐ tinfoil

☐ canvas   ☐ foil   ☐ thimble   ☐ wrapper

325. Objects (General Names)

Check (✔) the words you already know. Then, listen and repeat.

Tracks 1–2

☐ **object**

TR 1

☐ **thing**

TR 2

Definitions

An **object** is a thing that has a shape and that is not alive.

A **thing** is an object.

Check Your Understanding

A. Check (✔) all of the examples for each word.

1. thing
   - ☐ swimming
   - ☐ pizza
   - ☐ mother
   - ☐ television
   - ☐ ball

2. object
   - ☐ dog
   - ☐ door
   - ☐ toothbrush
   - ☐ fire
   - ☐ sister

B. Circle the correct answers to each question. Questions will have more than one answer.

1. What things might you use while cooking?

   bowl   paintbrush   spoon   oven   pots

2. What objects might you use in English class?

   teacher   dictionary   pen   classmate   air

3. What things might you use in gym class?

   ball   book   net   dog   bat

Challenge Words

Check (✔) the words you already know.

☐ entity   ☐ matter   ☐ substance

128

367. Packing and Wrapping

Check (✔) the words you already know. Then, listen and repeat.

 Tracks 1–4

☐ **tape**
TR 1

Definitions

When you **pack** a bag, you put clothes and other things into it, because you are going away.

If you **tape** one thing to another, you stick them together using tape.

If you **tie** something, you fasten it or fix it using string or a rope.

When you **wrap** something, you fold paper or cloth tightly around it to cover it.

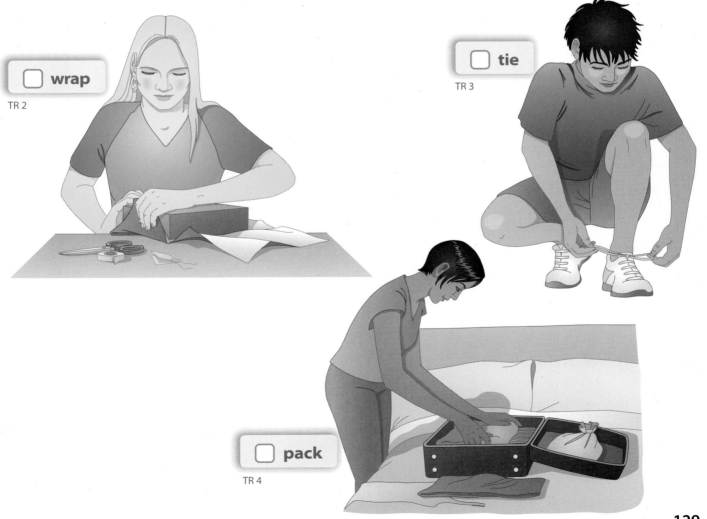

☐ **wrap**
TR 2

☐ **tie**
TR 3

☐ **pack**
TR 4

Check Your Understanding

A. Match each word to the correct description. One description will not be used.

1. _____ pack
2. _____ tape
3. _____ tie
4. _____ wrap

a. to fold paper around an object
b. to come apart in one long string
c. to put things into a bag or box
d. to use string to hold things together
e. to use a sticky piece of plastic to attach two things

B. Circle the correct answer.

1. Which of the following are you most likely to wrap?

a. your brother's telephone
b. your brother's dog
c. your brother's birthday present

2. Which of the following are you most likely to tape?

a. a broken window
b. a torn piece of paper
c. a torn pair of pants

3. Why would you pack something?

a. because you want to take it away
b. because you want to lose it
c. because you want to clean it

4. Which of the following would you tie?

a. your computer to the desk
b. a bow on a package
c. your car to the street

Challenge Words

Check (✔) the words you already know.

☐ bind ☐ furl ☐ unravel

98. General Names for Groups

Check (✔) the words you already know. Then, listen and repeat.

Tracks 1–10

☐ **gather**
TR 1

☐ **organize**
TR 2

Definitions

A **bunch** of things or people is a number of them that either grow or are placed together.

To **classify** things means to divide them into groups or types based on their similarities.

To **collect** means to bring items together from several places or several people.

To **gather** means to come together in a group.

A **group** of people or things is a number of people or things that are together.

To **list** names or other things means to write or say them one after another.

To **organize** means to plan or arrange items in a neat way.

A **pile** of things is several of them lying on top of each other.

A **sequence** of events or things is a number of them that come one after another.

To **stack** means to arrange things in a pile.

☐ **bunch**
TR 3

☐ **stack**
TR 4

☐ **collect**
TR 5

☐ **list**
TR 6

☐ **classify**
TR 7

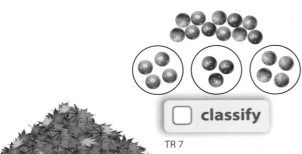

☐ **pile**
TR 8

1, 2, 3, 4, 5, 6, 7, 8, 9
A, B, C, D, E, F, G, H, I

☐ **sequence**
TR 9

☐ **group**
TR 10

Check Your Understanding

A. Underline the correct word to complete each sentence.

1. The friends (**gathered** / **stacked**) around the fire to hear a story.

2. For the class project, I am working in a (**group** / **pile**) with three other students.

3. After the party, there was a (**pile** / **bunch**) of plates on top of one another in the sink.

4. The classrooms are numbered in (**sequence** / **bunch**) from Room 1 to Room 20.

5. I picked a (**bunch** / **group**) of flowers for my grandmother.

6. During science class, we will (**classify** / **pile**) the animals into groups based on their size.

7. Our math teacher (**collects** / **stacks**) our homework each morning.

8. Jill (**listed** / **collected**) the names of the people that she was inviting to the party.

9. You should (**organize** / **list**) your papers by putting them into folders.

10. The movers (**stacked** / **classified**) the boxes by the door.

B. Write **T** for **true statements** and **F** for **false statements**.

1. _____ Your family might gather around the television to watch it together.

2. _____ If you are in a group, you are doing something with other people.

3. _____ When you hang your clothes in your closet, they are in a pile.

4. _____ If things happen in a sequence, they all happen at the same time.

5. _____ If you have a bunch of work to do, you have very little work.

6. _____ You can classify pets into different groups.

7. _____ When trash is collected, somebody picks up the trash from everyone on your street.

8. _____ If you have a lot of things to do, it is a good idea to list them.

9. _____ When somebody organizes a room, she cleans it and puts items into their proper place.

10. _____ Your teacher might stack your classmates to be more organized.

Challenge Words

Check (✔) the words you already know.

☐ arrange   ☐ assortment   ☐ collection   ☐ heap   ☐ schedule   ☐ summarize

☐ assemble   ☐ batch   ☐ file   ☐ menu   ☐ series   ☐ table

200. Social and Political Groups

Check (✔) the words you already know. Then, listen and repeat.

Tracks 1–8

☐ **family**
TR 1

☐ **race**
TR 2

☐ **democracy**
TR 3

☐ **community**
TR 4

☐ **nation**
TR 5

☐ **country**
TR 6

☐ **society**
TR 7

Definitions

A **community** is a group of people who are similar in some ways, or who have similar interests.

A **country** is an area of the world with its own government and people.

A **democracy** is a form of government in which people choose leaders to represent them.

A **family** is a group of people who are closely related to each other, and usually includes parents and their children.

A **nation** is an independent country with its own government, or a group of people living in and having a common loyalty to a country or region.

A **race** is one of the major groups that humans can be divided into according to their physical features, such as the color of their skin, their eyes, their hair, and so forth.

Society consists of a large group of people who share some of the same background and culture.

The word **tribe** is sometimes used for talking about a group of people of the same race, language, and culture, especially in a developing country. Some people disapprove of the use of this word.

☐ **tribe**
TR 8

Check Your Understanding

A. Choose the correct word from the word bank to complete each sentence.

family	democracy	race	tribe
country	community	nations	society

1. Most of my _____ lives nearby, but my brother moved out of state last year.

2. The people of the ancient _____ made tools that are now in the museum.

3. In that country, the leader has total power, but most people there want a _____ where they elect their leader.

4. In today's _____, most people get their information from television or the Internet.

5. In the United States, the Hispanic population is growing faster than that of any other _____.

6. Sylvie speaks French, and she is from the _____ of France.

7. People from many _____ came to the meeting on global issues.

8. Tonight, people from around the city are gathering for a _____ meeting.

B. Underline the correct word to complete each sentence.

1. Many people of Native American (**tribes / democracies**) died when they were exposed to new illnesses from Europe.

2. On the U.S. Census, people are asked to say to what (**tribe / race**) they belong to.

3. Have you ever traveled outside of our (**family / country**)?

4. I am so happy that we live in a (**tribe / democracy**) where citizens choose the members of the government.

5. In modern (**society / race**), many people spend a lot of time watching television.

6. Can you tell me the capital of the (**nation / family**) of Haiti?

7. I have a very large (**family / country**). I have three brothers and two sisters.

8. After the fire, everyone in our (**community / country**) helped the victims with food and clothes.

Challenge Words

Check (✔) the words you already know.

- ☐ civilization
- ☐ clan
- ☐ congress
- ☐ culture
- ☐ federal
- ☐ international
- ☐ national
- ☐ republic

258. Groups of Animals / People

Check (✔) the words you already know. Then, listen and repeat.

 Tracks 1–6

☐ **band**
TR 1

Definitions

A **band** is a group of people who play music together.

A **class** is a group of students who learn at school together.

A **club** is an organization of people who all like doing a particular activity.

A **crowd** is a large group of people who have gathered together.

A **herd** is a large group of one type of animal that lives together.

A **team** is a group of people who play a particular sport or game against other groups of people.

☐ **club**
TR 2

☐ **crowd**
TR 3

☐ **team**
TR 4

☐ **class**
TR 5

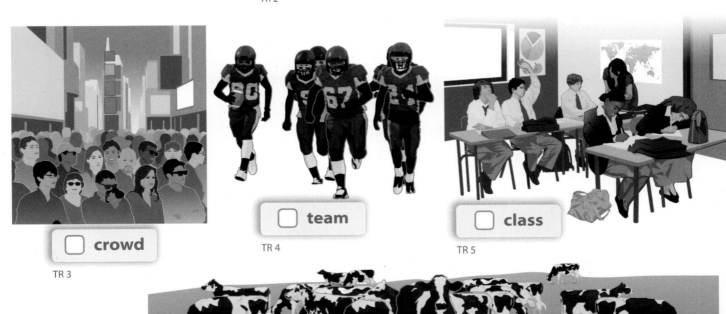

☐ **herd**
TR 6

Check Your Understanding

A. Circle the correct word to complete each sentence.

1. A large group of goats standing together on a hill is a _____.
   a. herd   b. class   c. band

2. The students who study science with you at the same time and with the same teacher are part of your _____.
   a. club   b. team   c. class

3. A group of people who play music together is called a _____.
   a. crowd   b. band   c. herd

4. If you really like to do math, you might see if there is a math _____ at your school.
   a. herd   b. crowd   c. club

5. If a famous athlete comes to speak at your school, there will certainly be a large _____.
   a. class   b. band   c. crowd

6. To have a baseball _____, you need at least nine people.
   a. team   b. herd   c. band

B. Circle the sentence that best matches each statement.

1. I play basketball with other people.
   a. I am on a team.   b. I am in a herd.

2. I am surrounded by people on all sides.
   a. I am in a club.   b. I am in a crowd.

3. I play the guitar, and my friends play the drums and the piano with me.
   a. We are in a band.   b. We are in a herd.

4. I see about 20 horses running together.
   a. I see a club.   b. I see a herd.

5. I am in a room with many other students and a teacher.
   a. I am in a class.   b. I am on a team.

6. I am part of a small group that learns to garden after school.
   a. I am in a gardening club.   b. I am in a gardening crowd.

Challenge Words

Check (✔) the words you already know.

- [ ] cast
- [ ] crew
- [ ] gang
- [ ] mob
- [ ] trio
- [ ] chorus
- [ ] flock
- [ ] huddle
- [ ] quartet

44 GROUPS

298. Military / Police

Check (✔) the words you already know. Then, listen and repeat.

 Tracks 1–3

Definitions

An **army** is a large group of soldiers who are trained to fight battles on land.

A country's **navy** is the military force that can fight at sea, and the ships they use.

The **police** is the organization that is responsible for making sure that people obey the law.

☐ **army**

TR 1

☐ **police**

TR 2

☐ **navy**

TR 3

Check Your Understanding

A. Write **T** for **true statements** and **F** for **false statements**.

1. _____ The police make sure that people follow the law.

2. _____ People in the army are trained to work on ships.

3. _____ If you join the navy, you will spend a lot of your time on the ocean.

4. _____ The police usually do their work on the ocean.

5. _____ People in the navy are mostly trained to fight on land.

6. _____ If you want to help to protect your country, you might join the army.

B. Match each group to the job that it does. One job will not be used.

1. _____ army   a. protect citizens of a community by making sure that they follow the law

2. _____ navy   b. protect citizens of a country by fighting battles in the air

3. _____ police   c. protect citizens of a country by fighting battles on land

                d. protect citizens of a country by fighting battles on the water

Challenge Words

Check (✔) the words you already know.

- ☐ air force
- ☐ brigade
- ☐ corps
- ☐ detail
- ☐ infantry
- ☐ legion
- ☐ marines
- ☐ patrol
- ☐ regiment
- ☐ troop

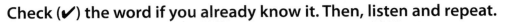

401. Business and Social Groups

Check (✔) the word if you already know it. Then, listen and repeat.

Track 1

☐ **audience**

TR 1

Definition

The **audience** of a performance, movie, or television program is all of the people who are watching or listening to it.

Check Your Understanding

A. Check (✔) each activity during which you would have an **audience**.

☐ surfing the Internet

☐ playing baseball on your school's team

☐ sleeping

☐ singing in a concert

☐ eating your lunch

☐ dancing in a ballet

☐ giving a presentation of your science project

B. Write **T** for **true statements** and **F** for **false statements**.

1. _____ When you are taking a test, you usually have a large audience.

2. _____ If you are playing in a basketball game at your school, there is probably an audience.

3. _____ If you go to a concert to see your favorite musical group, you are part of the audience.

Challenge Words

Check (✔) the words you already know.

☐ assembly   ☐ committee   ☐ convention   ☐ membership   ☐ staff

☐ association   ☐ company   ☐ league   ☐ organization   ☐ union

179. Recreational Events and Festivals

Check (✔) the words you already know. Then, listen and repeat.

Tracks 1–9

☐ birthday TR 2

☐ holiday TR 3

☐ date TR 6

☐ party TR 7

☐ vacation TR 1

Check Your Understanding

A. Choose the correct word from the word bank to complete each sentence.

party	fair	parade
recess	date	holidays
birthday	circus	vacation

1. New Year's Day and Independence Day are _____ that are celebrated in many countries, even if they're not always on the same days.

2. There were over 30 people at Lisa's _____ .

3. Darryl just got back from his _____ in Hawaii.

4. My sister and I are twins, so we share a _____ .

5. When the school bell rings, it is time to come inside from _____ .

6. Do you know if the _____ will go through the city park?

7. I saw a seal balancing a ball on its nose at the _____ .

8. I knew that Pete had a _____ tonight, but I did not know that it was with Katie.

9. People come from all over the county to have fun at the _____ .

B. Circle the correct word to complete each sentence.

1. I think that the bank is closed today because it is a _____ .

   a. circus   b. date   c. holiday

2. Kevin is dressed up for his _____ with Bridget.

   a. parade   b. date   c. birthday

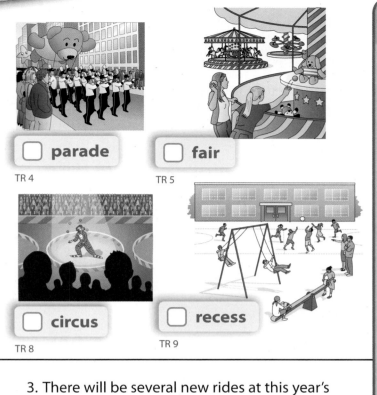

☐ parade
TR 4

☐ fair
TR 5

☐ circus
TR 8

☐ recess
TR 9

Definitions

Your **birthday** is the day of the year that you were born.

A **circus** is a group of people and animals that travels around to different places and performs shows.

A **date** is an arrangement to meet a boyfriend or a girlfriend.

A **fair** is a place where you can play games to win prizes, and you can ride on special, big machines for fun.

A **holiday** is a day when people do not go to work or school because of a religious or national celebration.

A **parade** is a line of people or vehicles moving through a public place in order to celebrate an important event.

A **party** is a social event at which people enjoy themselves doing things such as eating or dancing.

In a school, **recess** is the period of time when the children are allowed to play.

A **vacation** is a period of time when you relax and enjoy yourself, often away from home.

3. There will be several new rides at this year's state _____ .

   a. recess   b. holiday   c. fair

4. The mayor is marching in the _____ through the town's streets.

   a. parade   b. birthday   c. vacation

5. Mom and Dad want to take a _____ to the Grand Canyon this summer.

   a. party   b. vacation   c. recess

6. Is the _____ at your house tonight?

   a. party   b. circus   c. fair

7. All the children wish they had more than fifteen minutes for _____ .

   a. fairs   b. birthdays   c. recess

8. We bought tickets to go see the _____ .

   a. holiday   b. circus   c. vacation

9. Marie brought in cupcakes to celebrate Chris's _____ .

   a. fair   b. birthday   c. recess

Challenge Words

Check (✔) the words you already know.

☐ amusement   ☐ carnival   ☐ festival   ☐ pageant   ☐ prom

☐ anniversary   ☐ ceremony   ☐ honeymoon   ☐ pastime

412. Events and Dates (General)

Check (✔) the word if you already know it. Then, listen and repeat.

Track 1

Definition

An **event** is an organized activity or celebration.

☐ **event**

TR 1

Check Your Understanding

A. Check (✔) each event that might be organized by your school.

☐ a homework assignment

☐ a soccer game against another school

☐ a concert performed by the school band

☐ a daily trip home on the school bus

☐ an art show

B. Write **T** for **true statements** and **F** for **false statements**.

1. _____ Graduation is an important event for students.

2. _____ A school dance is a social event.

3. _____ Events can only happen on the weekend.

Challenge Words

Check (✔) the words you already know.

☐ affair   ☐ development   ☐ happening   ☐ occasion   ☐ project

☐ circumstance   ☐ experience   ☐ incident   ☐ occurrence   ☐ situation

413. Political Events

Check (✔) the word if you already know it. Then, listen and repeat.

Track 1

☐ **vote**
TR 1

Definition

To **vote** means to choose a specific person, rule, or law. You can **vote** for a leader, such as a president. Or, you can **vote** to show that you support or do not support a new rule or law.

Check Your Understanding

A. Check (✔) the jobs that people get because others **voted** for them.

☐ teacher   ☐ baseball player   ☐ president

☐ mayor   ☐ doctor   ☐ student

B. Circle the correct answer.

1. When you vote, you _____.
   a. choose the best person for a job
   b. attend a class
   c. visit the library

2. People vote in order to _____.
   a. figure things out for themselves
   b. choose actions or leaders
   c. make their lives more difficult

3. If you vote for a class president, you _____.
   a. choose the best student for the job
   b. choose the best teacher for the job
   c. choose the best parent for the job

Challenge Words

Check (✔) the words you already know.

☐ ballot   ☐ campaign   ☐ elect   ☐ nominate   ☐ voter

133. Soil

Check (✔) the words you already know. Then, listen and repeat.

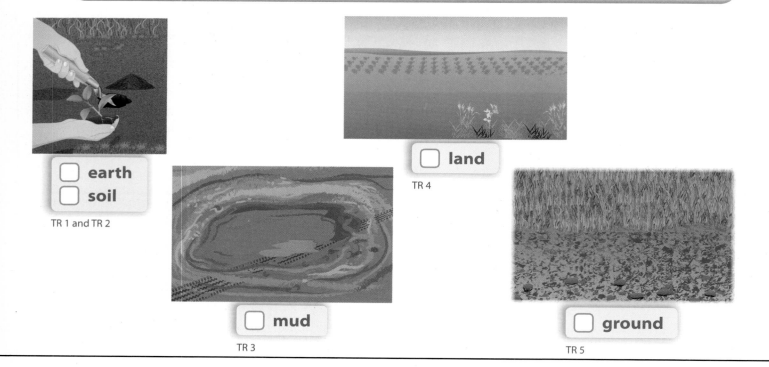

☐ **earth**
☐ **soil**

TR 1 and TR 2

☐ **land**

TR 4

☐ **mud**

TR 3

☐ **ground**

TR 5

Check Your Understanding

A. Underline the correct word to complete each sentence.

1. What a lovely vase! I did not know that you could use (**earth / clay**) to make such beautiful things.

2. Devon wants to plant his garden on the hill, but the (**dust / earth**) is too rocky.

3. Do we have enough (**soil / land**) to fill these flower pots?

4. After walking through the puddle, Jane's shoes were covered in (**land / mud**).

5. Peter got (**ground / dirt**) on his shirt right after he put it on.

6. All this (**land / soil**) was given to the city for a park.

7. The car made the (**dust / land**) fly into the air as it drove on the old road.

8. Why are all of those people sitting on the (**soil / ground**) when there are chairs right here?

☐ dirt
TR 6

☐ clay
TR 7

☐ dust
TR 8

Definitions

Clay is a type of earth that is soft when it is wet and hard when it is dry. Clay is used for making things such as pots and bricks.

Loose soil or earth is called **dirt**.

Dust is fine dry particles of earth or dirt.

Earth is the soil in which plants grow.

The **ground** is the surface of Earth.

Land is an area of ground, especially one that is used for a particular purpose such as farming or building.

Mud is a sticky mixture of earth and water.

Soil is the substance on the surface of the Earth in which plants grow.

B. Write **T** for **true statements** and **F** for **false statements**.

1. _____ Dirt is a sticky mixture of earth and water.

2. _____ When it doesn't rain for a long time, the earth turns to mud.

3. _____ You need to have good soil to grow flowers and vegetables.

4. _____ When you drop something on the ground, it might get dirt on it.

5. _____ You put seeds into clay to make plants grow.

6. _____ Dust is made up of large rocks.

7. _____ Your school was built on land.

8. _____ If you dig, you take earth out of the ground.

Challenge Words

Check (✔) the words you already know.

☐ manure   ☐ peat   ☐ sod   ☐ turf

145

237. Rocks and Jewels

Check (✔) the words you already know. Then, listen and repeat.

☐ **rock**
TR 2

☐ **diamond**
TR 4

☐ **boulder**
TR 1

☐ **jewel**
TR 3

Check Your Understanding

A. Circle the correct word to complete each sentence.

1. The walls in our garden are made of _____ .

   a. jewels   b. boulders   c. stone

2. Those earrings are very pretty, but very expensive. What _____ are in them?

   a. marble   b. jewels   c. rocks

3. There was a large _____ blocking the path in the forest, so we had to turn back.

   a. boulder   b. diamond   c. marble

4. This statue is highly detailed. The _____ must have been cut very carefully.

   a. jewel   b. marble   c. boulder

5. The ring that Patricia's husband gave her is a beautiful _____ .

   a. rock   b. marble   c. diamond

6. There are too many _____ in the ground here to plant anything.

   a. rocks   b. jewels   c. diamonds

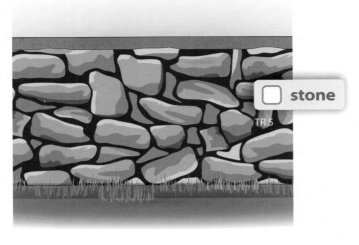

stone
TR 5

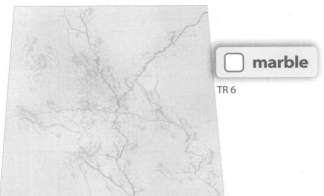

marble
TR 6

Definitions

A **boulder** is a large, round rock.

A **diamond** is a hard, clear stone that is very expensive and is used for making jewelry.

A **jewel** is a valuable stone, such as a diamond or a ruby.

Marble is a type of very hard rock that people use to make parts of buildings, floors, or statues.

A **rock** is a hard substance that is found in the ground and in mountains.

A **stone** is a hard, solid substance that is found in the ground and is often used for building.

B. Underline the correct word to complete each sentence.

1. Andy had several (**rocks / boulders**) from the beach in his pocket.

2. What beautiful earrings! Are those (**rocks / diamonds**) real?

3. This morning, the workers laid the first (**stone / diamond**) for our new patio.

4. How will we ever move this (**jewel / boulder**) from our yard?

5. Isabelle must be very rich. She is always wearing fine (**jewels / rocks**).

6. The mansion had several fireplaces, each of them made of (**boulder / marble**).

Challenge Words

Check (✔) the words you already know.

☐ coal ☐ crystal ☐ gem ☐ gravel ☐ ruby

☐ cobblestone ☐ emerald ☐ granite ☐ pearl ☐ slate

259. Metals

Check (✔) the words you already know. Then, listen and repeat.

Tracks 1–6

☐ **iron**

TR 1

☐ **gold**

TR 3

☐ **magnet**

TR 2

☐ **silver**

TR 4

Check Your Understanding

A. Circle the metal that would most likely be used in each situation.

1. You put a fence up around your house.

   magnet   silver   iron

2. You are wearing a necklace.

   iron   gold   magnet

3. You are wearing earrings.

   steel   silver   magnet

4. You need to hang a note on your refrigerator.

   metal   magnet   silver

5. People are working on a new building.

   silver   magnet   steel

6. You are wearing braces on your teeth.

   magnet   metal   gold

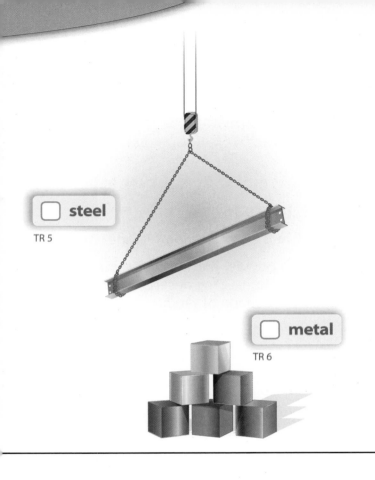

steel
TR 5

metal
TR 6

B. Match each word to the correct description. One description will not be used.

1. _____ gold
2. _____ iron
3. _____ magnet
4. _____ metal
5. _____ silver
6. _____ steel

a. a type of metal that attracts other metals, such as iron

b. gold, silver, steel, or iron

c. a metal that is used to make fancy forks, knives, and spoons

d. a yellow metal that is very valuable

e. a thin sheet of shiny paper used in baking

f. a strong metal made of iron that is used to make many things, such as cars

g. a dark, hard metal that is used to make steel

Challenge Words

Check (✔) the words you already know.

☐ alloy   ☐ brass   ☐ chrome   ☐ graphite

☐ aluminum   ☐ bronze   ☐ copper   ☐ lead

337. Characteristics of Rocks / Soil

Check (✔) the words you already know. Then, listen and repeat.

Tracks 1–2

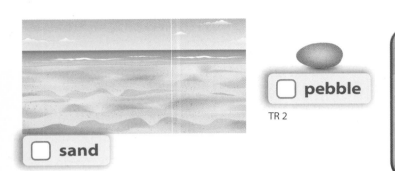

☐ sand

TR 1

☐ pebble

TR 2

Definitions

A **pebble** is a small, smooth stone.

Sand is a powder made of very small pieces of stone. Some deserts and most beaches are made of sand.

Check Your Understanding

A. Choose the correct word from the word bank to complete each sentence. Each word will be used twice.

sand	pebbles

1. While at the beach, Andy buried his hands in the _____.

2. Claire picked up a few _____ from her driveway.

3. The riverbed is covered with small _____, and they hurt my bare feet.

4. When we returned from the beach, we had to wash all the _____ off our feet.

B. Write **T** for **true statements** and **F** for **false statements**.

1. _____ Some deserts are made of sand.

2. _____ A pebble is a large rock.

3. _____ A pebble is a powder made of stones.

4. _____ Sand is a small, smooth stone.

Challenge Words

Check (✔) the words you already know.

☐ barren   ☐ mineral   ☐ powder

402. Actions Associated with Crops / Soil

Check (✔) the word if you already know it. Then, listen and repeat.

Track 1

☐ **plant**

TR 1

Definition

When you **plant** something, you put it into the ground so that it will grow. You can **plant** seeds to grow fruits and vegetables, bushes, and trees.

Check Your Understanding

A. Check (✔) the things that you can **plant**.

☐ tomatoes

☐ milk

☐ carrots

☐ bread

☐ flowers

☐ cars

☐ grass

B. Write **T** for **true statements** and **F** for **false statements**.

1. _____ You might plant seeds in a pot or in the ground.

2. _____ You cannot plant flowers or trees outside.

3. _____ When you plant a seed, you hope that it grows.

4. _____ It is always dangerous to eat things that have been planted.

Challenge Words

Check (✔) the words you already know.

☐ cultivate   ☐ harvest   ☐ plow   ☐ tend

☐ fertilize   ☐ irrigate   ☐ sow   ☐ till

245. Birth, Life, and Death

Check (✔) the words you already know. Then, listen and repeat.

Tracks 1–9

☐ dead
TR 2

☐ alive
TR 4

☐ born
TR 6

☐ egg
TR 1

☐ die
TR 3

☐ live
TR 5

☐ hatch
TR 7

☐ life
TR 8

Check Your Understanding

A. Choose the sentence that correctly uses the underlined word.

1. a. After the storm, we found a <u>dead</u> tree in the middle of the forest.

   b. These plants are <u>dead</u> and will grow to be very tall.

2. a. The cat just stopped breathing. Now he is <u>alive</u>.

   b. The cat is still breathing. He is still <u>alive</u>.

3. a. The father held his baby as soon as it was <u>born</u>.

   b. The father held his baby before it was <u>born</u>.

4. a. Julie was sad for a long time after her dog <u>died</u>.

   b. Julie was happy for a long time after her dog <u>died</u>.

5. a. The baby cat spent several weeks in its <u>egg</u> before it came out.

   b. The baby bird spent several weeks in its <u>egg</u> before it came out.

6. a. John watched as his son <u>hatched</u> right before his eyes.

   b. John watched as the baby turtle <u>hatched</u> right before his eyes.

7. a. Victoria has had an interesting <u>life</u>, filled with adventure.

   b. Victoria has had an interesting <u>life</u> and was born yesterday.

8. a. That woman <u>lives</u> dangerously. She died in a car accident last week.

   b. That woman <u>lives</u> dangerously. She always does things where she could get hurt.

9. a. We went to the <u>wake</u> to celebrate the wedding.

   b. We went to the <u>wake</u> when our neighbor died.

☐ wake

TR 9

Definitions

When people or animals are **alive**, they are not dead.

To be **born** means to give someone or something life.

A person, animal, or plant that is **dead** has stopped living.

To **die** means to stop living.

An **egg** is a round or oval-shaped shell in which a baby bird, reptile, or insect grows.

To **hatch** means to come out of an egg.

Someone's **life** is their state of being alive, or the period of time when they are alive.

To **live** means to be alive.

A **wake** is a time to visit a dead person's body before burial.

B. Write **T** for **true statements** and **F** for **false statements**.

1. _____ On your birthday, you celebrate the day you were born.

2. _____ When a person dies, she is no longer alive.

3. _____ When a bird comes out of an egg, it hatches.

4. _____ When an animal comes out of its mother's body, you say it hatches.

5. _____ A person who was born in 1850 is dead today.

6. _____ A person who was born in 1850 is alive today.

7. _____ If a person lived for 100 years, he or she had a long life.

8. _____ A wake is a time when a new baby is born.

9. _____ If a person is breathing, that person is dead.

Challenge Words

Check (✔) the words you already know.

☐ animate   ☐ dwell   ☐ gene   ☐ mortal   ☐ reproduction

☐ birth   ☐ extinct   ☐ inhabit   ☐ populate   ☐ suffocate

153

329. Growth and Survival

Check (✔) the words you already know. Then, listen and repeat.

 Tracks 1–2

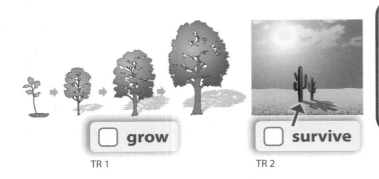

☐ grow

TR 1

☐ survive

TR 2

Definitions

To **grow** means to gradually become bigger.

To **survive** means to live or exist under very difficult conditions.

Check Your Understanding

A. Circle the correct example of each word.

1. grow
   a. Last year Charlie was five feet tall, and now he is five feet tall.
   b. Last year Charlie was five feet tall, and now he is six feet tall.
   c. Last year Charlie was six feet tall, and now he is six feet tall.

2. survive
   a. The plant did not grow because it needed more water.
   b. The leaves of the plant died in the hot sun.
   c. The plant lived through the cold, snowy winter.

B. Choose the correct word from the word bank to complete each sentence. Each word will be used twice.

grow	survived

1. If this tree continues to _____, it will be taller than the house!
2. The tree in my yard _____ the storm, but the flowers are completely ruined.
3. If I _____ any taller, my pants will be too short.
4. The people _____ the cold winter, even though they didn't have much food.

Challenge Words

Check (✔) the words you already know.

☐ bloom   ☐ evolve   ☐ mature   ☐ prosper   ☐ thrive

90. Nature and Weather (General)

Check (✔) the words you already know. Then, listen and repeat.

Tracks 1–3

Definitions

Air is the mixture of gases all around us that we breathe.

Nature is all the animals, plants, and other things in the world that are not made by people.

The **weather** is the temperature and conditions outside, for example, if it is raining, hot, or windy.

 air

TR 1

☐ **nature**

TR 2

☐ **weather**

TR 3

Check Your Understanding

A. Match each word to the correct description. Each word will have two answers.

1. _____ air
2. _____ weather
3. _____ nature

a. forest
b. rainy
c. sunny
d. mixture of gases
e. rabbits
f. something we breathe

B. Complete the story with correct word from the word bank.

air	weather	nature

My dad has always loved being in (1) _____ . He loves trees and animals. Every Sunday, if the (2) _____ is nice, he takes us to the lake. As soon as we get there, he runs down to the lake. He takes a big breath of fresh (3) _____ and says, "Wow, I love it out here!"

Challenge Words

Check (✔) the words you already know.

☐ atmosphere   ☐ climate   ☐ environment

226. Wind and Storms

Check (✔) the words you already know. Then, listen and repeat.

🎧 Tracks 1–10

☐ **storm**
TR 1

☐ **lightning**
TR 2

☐ **thunder**
TR 3

☐ **draft**
TR 4

☐ **downpour**
TR 5

Definitions

A **blizzard** is a very bad storm with snow and strong winds.

A **downpour** is a sudden, heavy rain.

A **draft** is cold air that comes into a room.

A **hurricane** is a storm with very strong winds and rain that usually forms over an ocean.

Lightning is a very bright flash of light in the sky that happens during a storm.

A **storm** is very bad weather, with heavy rain and strong winds.

Thunder is the loud noise that you sometimes hear from the sky during a storm.

A **thunderstorm** is a very noisy storm that usually has rain, thunder, and lightning.

A **tornado** is a storm with strong winds that spin around very fast and cause a lot of damage.

Wind is air that moves.

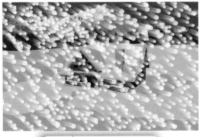

☐ **blizzard**
TR 6

☐ **tornado**
TR 7

☐ **wind**
TR 8

☐ **thunderstorm**
TR 9

☐ **hurricane**
TR 10

Check Your Understanding

A. Underline the correct word to complete each sentence.

1. Although the rain is light now, there may be a (**storm / draft**) this afternoon.

2. The (**thunder / wind**) is blowing sand everywhere.

3. The loud sound of the (**draft / thunder**) woke everyone up.

4. There is a lot of snow outside because of the (**downpour / blizzard**) last night.

5. The winds from the (**tornado / thunder**) caused a lot of damage to the homes in this area.

6. The weather report said that there is a (**hurricane / lightning**) forming over the ocean near Florida.

7. The (**lightning / thunder**) lit up the night sky.

8. The power went out during the (**draft / thunderstorm**).

9. I forgot my umbrella, so I got wet in the (**downpour / draft**).

10. Please make sure that the window is shut. There is a (**thunderstorm / draft**) coming in.

B. Match each word to the correct description. One description will not be used.

1. _____ storm	a. air that moves
2. _____ thunder	b. flashes of light in the sky
3. _____ blizzard	c. a very loud storm with rain, thunder, and lightning
4. _____ downpour	d. bad weather, usually with heavy rains and wind
5. _____ draft	e. a sudden, heavy rain
6. _____ hurricane	f. a storm with fast, turning winds
7. _____ lightning	g. cold air coming into a room
8. _____ thunderstorm	h. a large wind and rain storm that forms over the ocean
9. _____ tornado	i. a strong winter storm during which a lot of snow falls
10. _____ wind	j. the loud noise you hear during a storm
	k. a gentle wind

Challenge Words

Check (✔) the words you already know.

☐ breeze   ☐ gust   ☐ rainstorm   ☐ squall   ☐ twister

☐ cyclone   ☐ monsoon   ☐ snowstorm   ☐ thunderbolt   ☐ windstorm

307. Natural Catastrophes

Check (✔) the words you already know. Then, listen and repeat.

Tracks 1–3

☐ **avalanche**

TR 1

Definitions

An **avalanche** is a large amount of snow or rocks and dirt that falls down the side of a mountain.

An **earthquake** is when the ground shakes because Earth's surface is moving.

If there is a **flood,** a lot of water covers land that is usually dry.

☐ **earthquake**

TR 2

☐ **flood**

TR 3

159

Check Your Understanding

A. Read each description. Then write whether it describes an **avalanche**, an **earthquake**, or a **flood.**

1. _____ The water was almost six feet high!

2. _____ The ice, snow, and rocks rolled onto the cars below.

3. _____ The ground shook for about ten seconds.

4. _____ The entire house was covered in snow, and people were trapped inside.

5. _____ It had rained for days, and water was coming up out of the river.

B. Write **T** for **true statements** and **F** for **false statements.**

1. _____ During an avalanche, snow stays on a mountain.

2. _____ If there is a flood in your basement, there is water everywhere.

3. _____ A strong earthquake can knock a building over.

4. _____ Normally, floods occur after a little rain falls.

5. _____ An avalanche might occur in the summertime, at the beach.

Challenge Words

Check (✔) the words you already know.

- [ ] calamity
- [ ] crisis
- [ ] disastrous
- [ ] landslide
- [ ] tragedy
- [ ] catastrophe
- [ ] disaster
- [ ] emergency
- [ ] ordeal

375. Characteristics Associated with Weather

Check (✔) the words you already know. Then, listen and repeat.

Tracks 1–3

☐ **dry**

TR 1

Definitions

If the weather is **dry**, there is no rain.

If the sky is **overcast**, it is completely covered with clouds.

When it is **sunny**, the sun shines brightly.

☐ **overcast**

TR 2

☐ **sunny**

TR 3

Check Your Understanding

A. Choose the word from the word bank that best matches each statement. You will use some words more than once.

dry	overcast	sunny

1. _____ It hasn't rained in two months.

2. _____ The grass is turning brown because there is no rain.

3. _____ The sky is full of gray clouds.

4. _____ The sun is shining so brightly.

5. _____ It looks like it might rain.

B. Match each action to each type of weather. One action will not be used.

1. _____ dry   a. open an umbrella

2. _____ overcast   b. wear sunglasses

3. _____ sunny   c. water the grass and plants

                                    d. bring a raincoat to school

Challenge Words

Check (✔) the words you already know.

☐ arid   ☐ muggy   ☐ sultry

406. Clouds

Check (✔) the word if you already know it. Then, listen and repeat.

Track 1

TR 1

☐ cloud

Definition

A **cloud** is a white or gray mass in the sky that contains drops of water.

Check Your Understanding

A. Circle the correct answer.

1. What colors are most clouds?

   a. red and blue   b. white and gray   c. yellow and white

2. Where do you see clouds?

   a. in the sky   b. on the ground   c. both *a* and *b*

3. What do gray clouds mean?

   a. It might rain.   b. It is a sunny day.   c. It is windy.

4. What does it mean when there are no clouds in the sky?

   a. It is about to rain.   b. It is nighttime.   c. It is not going to rain.

B. Write **T** for **true statements** and **F** for **false statements**.

1. _____ When you see a few white clouds, you should carry an umbrella.

2. _____ If the sky looks gray, it is filled with clouds.

3. _____ An airplane might pass through the clouds.

4. _____ A car might pass through the clouds.

Challenge Words

Check (✔) the words you already know.

☐ cirrus   ☐ cumulus   ☐ thunderhead

185. Cleanliness / Hygiene

Check (✔) the words you already know. Then, listen and repeat.

Track 1–6

☐ **scrub**
TR 1

☐ **sweep**
TR 2

☐ **clean**
TR 3

Check Your Understanding

A. Circle the correct answer.

1. Robert had to _____ the floor after he broke the glass.

   a. wipe   b. sweep   c. rinse

2. Please use this napkin to _____ the chocolate off your mouth.

   a. rinse   b. sweep   c. wipe

3. Anna had to work hard to _____ the bathtub.

   a. scrub   b. sweep   c. rinse

4. As soon as we finish _____ the house, we can go out to lunch.

   a. rinsing   b. cleaning   c. wiping

5. The dog jumped out of the bathtub and got soap everywhere before we could _____ him.

   a. wipe   b. sweep   c. rinse

6. It is important to _____ your hands with soap and water before you start to cook.

   a. sweep   b. wash   c. wipe

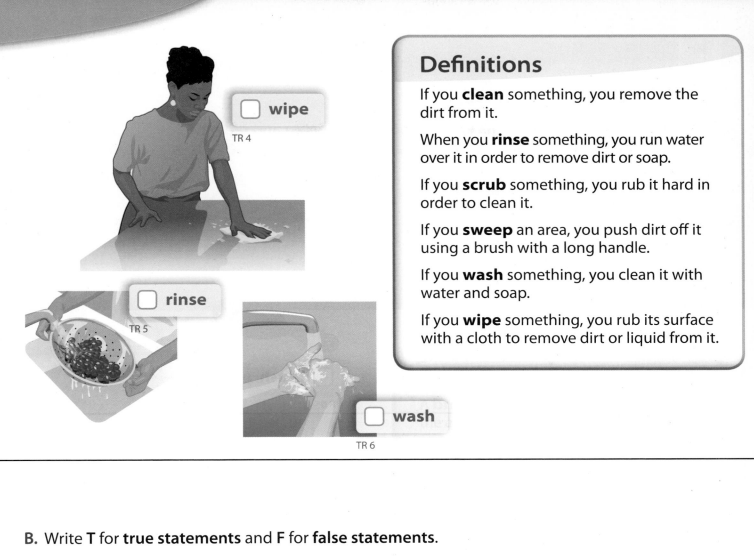

Definitions

If you **clean** something, you remove the dirt from it.

When you **rinse** something, you run water over it in order to remove dirt or soap.

If you **scrub** something, you rub it hard in order to clean it.

If you **sweep** an area, you push dirt off it using a brush with a long handle.

If you **wash** something, you clean it with water and soap.

If you **wipe** something, you rub its surface with a cloth to remove dirt or liquid from it.

B. Write **T** for **true statements** and **F** for **false statements**.

1. _____ You might clean your house by wiping furniture and floors with a cloth.

2. _____ If you wipe your hands, you put them under water to get the soap off them.

3. _____ It is good to rinse fruits and vegetables before you eat them.

4. _____ You might scrub your face with soap to get it clean.

5. _____ When you sweep the floor, you clean it with soap and water.

6. _____ After dinner, the dishes need to be washed.

Challenge Words

Check (✔) the words you already know.

☐ bathe	☐ filter	☐ immaculate	☐ polish	☐ scour
☐ buff	☐ hygiene	☐ manicure	☐ purge	☐ sterile

165

8. _____ suds

9. _____ toothbrush

10. _____ toothpaste

g. a substance that you use with water to wash people and things

h. a small piece of wood used to clean your teeth

i. a long string that is used to clean between teeth

j. a long stick with strings at the end that is used to wash floors

k. a small brush that is used to clean teeth

Challenge Words

Check (✔) the words you already know.

☐ bleach	☐ cleaner	☐ lather	☐ toothpick
☐ broom	☐ detergent	☐ lotion	☐ vacuum

167

223. Cleaning Tools

Check (✔) the words you already know. Then, listen and repeat.

 Tracks 1–10

 ☐ **soap**
TR 1

 ☐ **toothbrush**
TR 2

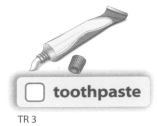 ☐ **toothpaste**
TR 3

 SHAMPOO

288. Uncleanliness and Filth

Check (✔) the words you already know. Then, listen and repeat.

 Tracks 1–4

☐ **litter** →
TR 1

Check Your Understanding

A. Circle the best example of each word.

1. garbage
   a. empty food cans and wrappers from things you have eaten
   b. cans and packages of food found at the grocery store

2. junk
   a. a new MP3 player that you took out of the box
   b. a broken MP3 player that you found on the street

3. litter
   a. a can on a kitchen counter
   b. a can on the sidewalk

4. trash
   a. used plastic cups from a party
   b. new plastic cups for a party

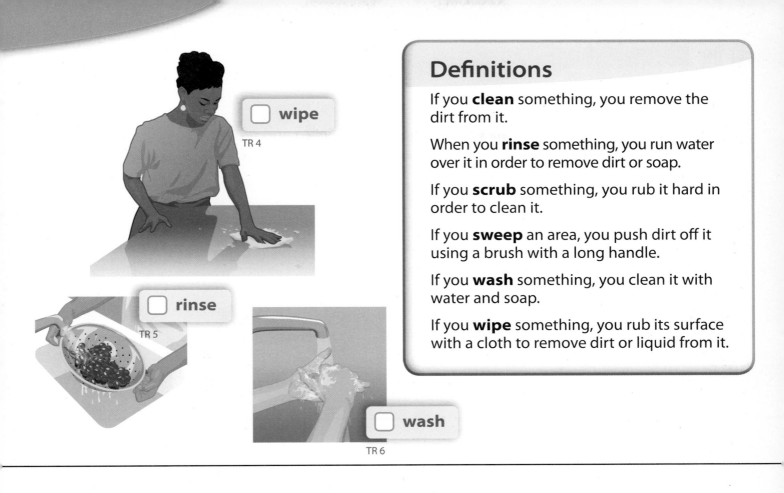

Definitions

If you **clean** something, you remove the dirt from it.

When you **rinse** something, you run water over it in order to remove dirt or soap.

If you **scrub** something, you rub it hard in order to clean it.

If you **sweep** an area, you push dirt off it using a brush with a long handle.

If you **wash** something, you clean it with water and soap.

If you **wipe** something, you rub its surface with a cloth to remove dirt or liquid from it.

wipe

TR 4

rinse

TR 5

wash

TR 6

B. Write T for true statements and F for false statements.

1. _____ You might clean your house by wiping furniture and floors with a cloth.

2. _____ If you wipe your hands, you put them under water to get the soap off them.

3. _____ It is good to rinse fruits and vegetables before you eat them.

4. _____ You might scrub your face with soap to get it clean.

5. _____ When you sweep the floor, you clean it with soap and water.

6. _____ After dinner, the dishes need to be washed.

Challenge Words

Check (✔) the words you already know.

- bathe
- buff
- filter
- hygiene
- immaculate
- manicure
- polish
- purge
- scour
- sterile

223. Cleaning Tools

Check (✔) the words you already know. Then, listen and repeat.

Tracks 1–10

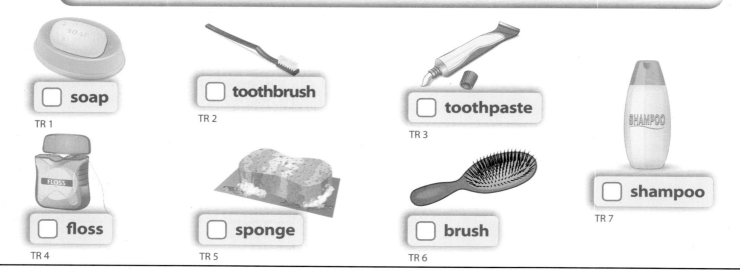

☐ soap
TR 1

☐ toothbrush
TR 2

☐ toothpaste
TR 3

☐ shampoo
TR 7

☐ floss
TR 4

☐ sponge
TR 5

☐ brush
TR 6

Check Your Understanding

A. Circle the correct word to complete each sentence.

1. I need the _____ to sweep up the cookie crumbs on the floor.
   a. brush   b. soap   c. broomstick

2. My dentist gave me a small tube of _____ at my last visit.
   a. toothbrush   b. toothpaste   c. suds

3. The wet dog was covered in _____ during his bath.
   a. suds   b. toothpaste   c. brush

4. Daniel said he needed a _____ to clean the spilled milk off the floor.
   a. floss   b. toothbrush   c. mop

5. My new _____ makes my hair smell like apples after I wash it.
   a. shampoo   b. sponge   c. toothpaste

6. Julie makes sure she uses a strong _____ on her hands to get them really clean.
   a. broomsticks   b. toothbrushes c. soap

7. After eating so much popcorn, I really needed some _____ to get it out of my teeth.
   a. sponges   b. floss   c. mops

8. Ellen used a _____ to wipe the chocolate off of her son's hands.
   a. toothbrush   b. broomstick   c. sponge

9. Katia's hair is so thick that she needs a very big, strong _____ to neaten it up in the morning.
   a. brush   b. toothbrush   c. shampoo

10. Don't forget to pack your _____ when you leave for vacation.
    a. toothbrush   b. mop   c. broomstick

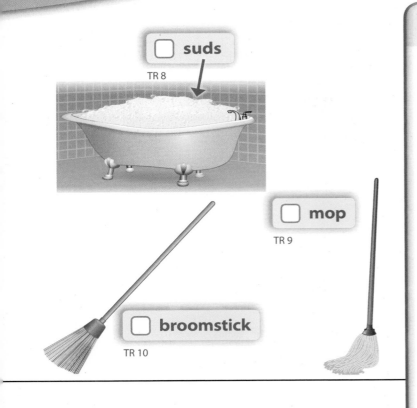

suds
TR 8

mop
TR 9

broomstick
TR 10

Definitions

A **broomstick** is a long stick with a brush at the end that is used to sweep floors.

You use a **brush** to make your hair neat or to clean objects.

Floss is a special type of string that you use to clean between your teeth.

A **mop** is a long stick with a lot of thick pieces of string at one end. It is used to wash floors.

Shampoo is a liquid soap you use to wash or clean your hair.

Soap is a substance that you use with water to wash yourself or your clothes.

A **sponge** is a piece of a very light, soft material with little holes in it. You use a sponge to wash yourself or to clean things.

Suds are the bubbles that soap makes in water.

A **toothbrush** is a small brush that you use to clean your teeth.

Toothpaste is a thick substance that you put on a toothbrush and use to clean your teeth.

B. Match each word to the correct description. One description will not be used.

1. _____ brush
2. _____ soap
3. _____ broomstick
4. _____ floss
5. _____ mop
6. _____ shampoo
7. _____ sponge
8. _____ suds
9. _____ toothbrush
10. _____ toothpaste

a. a thick substance that is used to clean teeth

b. a liquid soap that is used to clean hair

c. a small, hard object used to neaten your hair

d. a long stick with a brush at the end that is used to sweep floors

e. small bubbles that form when soap and water mix

f. a light, soft item with small holes used for cleaning

g. a substance that you use with water to wash people and things

h. a small piece of wood used to clean your teeth

i. a long string that is used to clean between teeth

j. a long stick with strings at the end that is used to wash floors

k. a small brush that is used to clean teeth

Challenge Words

Check (✔) the words you already know.

☐ bleach
☐ broom
☐ cleaner
☐ detergent
☐ lather
☐ lotion
☐ toothpick
☐ vacuum

288. Uncleanliness and Filth

Check (✔) the words you already know. Then, listen and repeat.

 Tracks 1–4

☐ **litter**

TR 1

Check Your Understanding

A. Circle the best example of each word.

1. garbage
   a. empty food cans and wrappers from things you have eaten
   b. cans and packages of food found at the grocery store

2. junk
   a. a new MP3 player that you took out of the box
   b. a broken MP3 player that you found on the street

3. litter
   a. a can on a kitchen counter
   b. a can on the sidewalk

4. trash
   a. used plastic cups from a party
   b. new plastic cups for a party

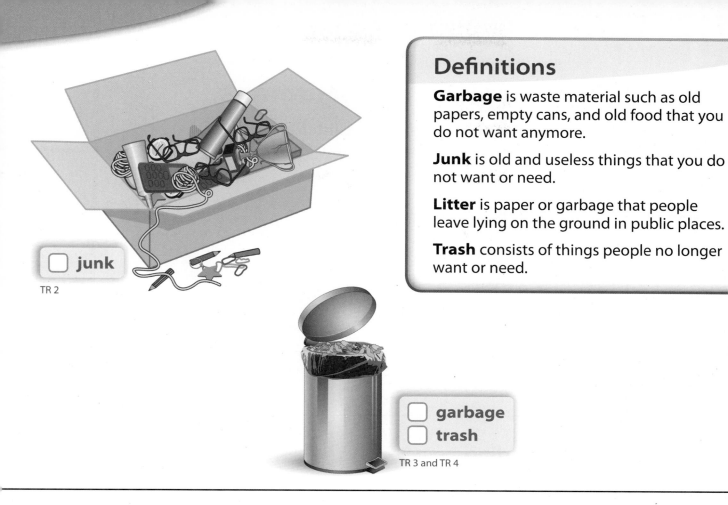

junk

TR 2

garbage

trash

TR 3 and TR 4

Definitions

Garbage is waste material such as old papers, empty cans, and old food that you do not want anymore.

Junk is old and useless things that you do not want or need.

Litter is paper or garbage that people leave lying on the ground in public places.

Trash consists of things people no longer want or need.

B. Choose the sentence that correctly uses the underlined word.

1. a. Every week, city workers pick up the garbage and take it away in a truck.

   b. Every week, city workers make new garbage and share it with the neighbors.

2. a. Look at all this junk—broken glasses, old toys, and empty jars.

   b. Look at all this junk—diamond rings, gold earrings, and a silver watch.

3. a. The principal liked it when she saw litter all over the soccer field.

   b. The principal got upset when she saw litter all over the soccer field.

4. a. I cannot fix that broken plate with glue. It is now trash.

   b. I bought lovely new plates yesterday. They are now trash.

Challenge Words

Check (✔) the words you already know.

bleak	debris	foul	infect	pollute
clutter	filth	grime	nasty	sewage

110. Actions Helpful to Humans

Check (✔) the words you already know. Then, listen and repeat.

Tracks 1–6

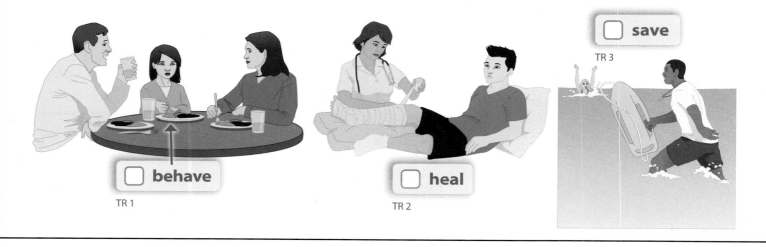

☐ save
TR 3

☐ behave
TR 1

☐ heal
TR 2

Check Your Understanding

A. Match each word to the best example. One example will not be used.

1. _____ behave
2. _____ help
3. _____ save
4. _____ heal
5. _____ improve
6. _____ protect

a. Will cut his grandmother's grass for her and cleaned out her garage.

b. Janie made a sandwich in her kitchen.

c. The policeman walks up and down the street to make sure nobody is causing harm.

d. Sally used to be a horrible painter, but she just won first place in the art show.

e. The students in the room listened closely to the speaker, and nobody was talking.

f. Nick dived into the water and pulled his cousin to safety.

g. The doctors operated on Dad a few months ago, and he is feeling better now.

help
TR 4

improve
TR 5

protect
TR 6

Definitions

To **behave** means to act in a way that people think is correct and proper.

When a broken bone or other injury **heals**, it becomes healthy again.

To **help** means to make it easier for a person to do something.

To **improve** means to get better.

To **protect** someone or something means to keep them safe from harm or damage.

To **save** someone or something means to help them to escape from a dangerous situation.

B. Choose the correct word from the word bank to complete each sentence.

help	heal	protect
behaved	saved	improved

1. Please wear this hat and gloves to _____ your body from the cold.

2. The children in this class _____ so well that the teacher gave them a treat.

3. The rescue team _____ the people trapped by the flood.

4. How long did the doctor say it will take for your broken leg to _____?

5. This neighborhood used to be very dangerous, but it has really _____ and is much safer.

6. Could you please _____ me bring these bags of groceries into the house?

Challenge Words

Check (✔) the words you already know.

☐ advantage   ☐ assist   ☐ cure   ☐ guide   ☐ refresh

☐ aid   ☐ benefit   ☐ defend   ☐ recover   ☐ rescue

161. Actions Harmful to Humans

Check (✔) the words you already know. Then, listen and repeat.

Tracks 1–7

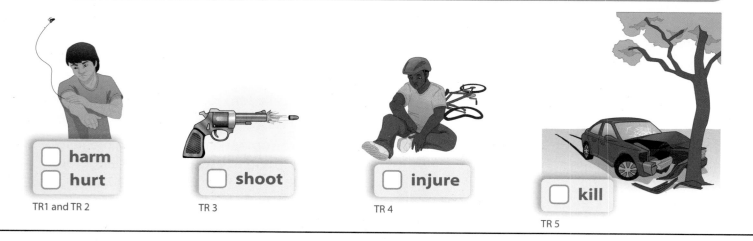

☐ harm			
☐ hurt	☐ shoot	☐ injure	☐ kill
TR1 and TR 2	TR 3	TR 4	TR 5

Check Your Understanding

A. Circle the best example of each word.

1. hurt

   a. a dentist pulling a tooth out of your mouth   b. a dentist checking your teeth

2. kill

   a. a mother lion licking her babies

   b. a mother lion hunting a small animal for her babies to eat

3. punish

   a. a parent giving his son a video game for getting good grades

   b. a parent taking video games away from his son because of his bad grades

4. harm

   a. smoking cigarettes

   b. teaching children about the dangers of cigarettes

5. injure

   a. jumping off of a diving board into water

   b. falling off of a bicycle and scraping your knee

6. murder

   a. getting angry and killing someone

   b. hitting a bird with a car by accident

7. shoot

   a. using an arrow to kill an animal   b. using a knife to kill an animal

No television for one week.

☐ punish

TR 6

☐ murder

TR 7

Definitions

To **harm** someone means to injure or damage that person.

To **hurt** means to cause someone to feel pain.

To **injure** means to damage a part of your body.

To **kill** means to cause the death of any living thing.

To **murder** someone means to kill them on purpose.

To **punish** is to discipline or to make someone pay for doing something wrong.

To **shoot** someone means to kill or injure another person by firing a gun or shooting an arrow.

B. Underline the correct word to complete each sentence.

1. Matt (**injured / punished**) his arm in an accident at work.

2. The plane crash (**shot / killed**) everybody on the airplane.

3. Our parents (**punished / injured**) us by sending us to our rooms when we behaved badly.

4. All these chemicals are going to (**shoot / harm**) the people who eat this food.

5. The doctor said the shot was not going to (**hurt / punish**), but it did.

6. Andy knows how to (**shoot / harm**) an arrow and hit the target.

7. In this movie, the man is on trial for (**murdering / punishing**) someone during a robbery.

Challenge Words

Check (✔) the words you already know.

☐ assault ☐ deadly ☐ offend ☐ penalty ☐ torment

☐ attack ☐ discipline ☐ painful ☐ stun ☐ torture

250. Destructive Actions

Check (✔) the words you already know. Then, listen and repeat.

 Tracks 1–12

☐ scratch
TR 1

☐ destroy
TR 2

☐ dent
TR 4

☐ crash
TR 5

☐ accident
TR 6

☐ damage
TR 8

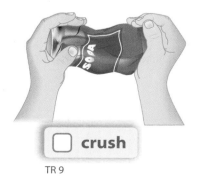
☐ crush
TR 9

☐ break
TR 10

wreck
TR 3

mark
TR 7

Definitions

When there is an **accident**, something bad happens by chance, sometimes causing injury or death.

To **break** something means to separate it into two or more pieces, often because you have dropped it or hit it.

To **crash** means to hit a person or thing.

To **crush** something means to press it very hard so that it breaks or loses its shape.

To **damage** something means to break it or harm it.

To **dent** the surface of something means to make a hollow area in it by hitting it with another object.

To **destroy** something means to cause so much damage to it that it cannot be used any longer, or does not exist any longer.

To **mark** something means to make a spot or a stain on it.

To **ruin** something means to completely harm, damage, or spoil it so that it cannot be used anymore.

To **scratch** means to make small cuts on the surface of something.

To **waste** something means to make poor use, or no use, of something valuable.

To **wreck** something means to completely destroy or ruin it.

ruin
TR 11

waste
TR 12

175

Check Your Understanding

A. Underline the correct word to complete each sentence.

1. A baseball from the nearby park (**dented / destroyed**) the top of my car.

2. Wally (**crushed / crashed**) all the cans before he took them to the recycling center.

3. The horrible fire spread through the town and (**destroyed / crashed**) many homes.

4. Please put the cap on the marker so that it does not (**mark / break**) the table.

5. My sister (**crashed / ruined**) my white skirt when she spilled juice on it.

6. Somebody used a key to (**break / scratch**) the side of Jean's car.

7. Mom gave us each 20 dollars for the movies, but I (**broke / wasted**) all the money on candy.

8. The strong winds (**wasted / damaged**) several homes in the area.

9. The other car drove through the stop sign and (**crushed / crashed**) right into our car.

10. Where did the automobile (**accident / mark**) happen?

11. Nobody knows who (**wasted / broke**) the vase.

12. Three weeks after he got his new car, he (**scratched / wrecked**) it by hitting a tree.

B. Write **T** for **true statements** and **F** for **false statements**.

1. _____ When your car is scratched, you cannot drive it safely.

2. _____ If you eat all the food on your plate, you waste it.

3. _____ When you get hurt in an accident, you did not mean for it to happen.

4. _____ If you break something, you put several pieces of that thing together.

5. _____ If a train wrecks, it reaches its destination safely.

6. _____ If you spill tomato sauce on a white shirt, it may leave a mark.

7. _____ A book is completely ruined if one of its pages is folded.

8. _____ If you crush a plant by stepping on it, you damage it.

9. _____ If you destroy your computer, you cannot use it anymore.

10. _____ If you drop something heavy onto your car, it might dent it.

11. _____ When two cars park next to each other, they crash.

12. _____ If you damage something, you make it better.

Challenge Words

Check (✔) the words you already know.

- [ ] chip
- [ ] demolish
- [ ] devastate
- [ ] erase
- [ ] extinguish
- [ ] fracture
- [ ] mash
- [ ] puncture
- [ ] shatter
- [ ] wreckage

260. War and Fighting

Check (✔) the words you already know. Then, listen and repeat.

Tracks 1-6

☐ **wrestle**

TR 1

☐ **peace**

TR 2

☐ **revolution**

TR 3

Check Your Understanding

A. Choose the correct word from the word bank to complete each sentence.

battle	peace	war
fighting	revolution	wrestled

1. The soldiers who won the last _____ will set the terms for the end of the war.

2. Sam's team won the match after he _____ his opponent to the ground.

3. Tim and Marcia are _____. I don't think they have spoken in days.

4. The leaders of the _____ are hoping to bring change to their country.

5. Everybody in the country wanted the _____ to end.

6. When there is no war, there is _____.

□ fight
TR 5

□ war
TR 4

□ battle
TR 6

Definitions

A **battle** is a violent fight between groups of people, especially between armies during a war.

When people **fight**, they try to hurt each other with words, weapons, or physical force.

When there is **peace** in a country, there is no war.

A **revolution** is an attempt by a group of people to change their country's government by using force.

A **war** is a period of fighting between countries or groups.

When you **wrestle** with someone, you fight by trying to throw that person to the ground.

B. Match each word to the correct description. One description will not be used.

1. _____ battle
2. _____ fight
3. _____ peace
4. _____ revolution
5. _____ war
6. _____ wrestle

a. a period with no war

b. a fight that takes place during a war

c. to fight and try to throw a person to the ground

d. to have a conflict or argument

e. a period without peace

f. when a group of people organizes to change their government

g. an event in which a group of people gets out of control

Challenge Words

Check (✔) the words you already know.

☐ challenge   ☐ combat   ☐ invade   ☐ scuffle   ☐ struggle

☐ clash   ☐ conflict   ☐ riot   ☐ showdown   ☐ warfare

221. Ease and Difficulty

Check (✔) the words you already know. Then, listen and repeat.

Tracks 1–4

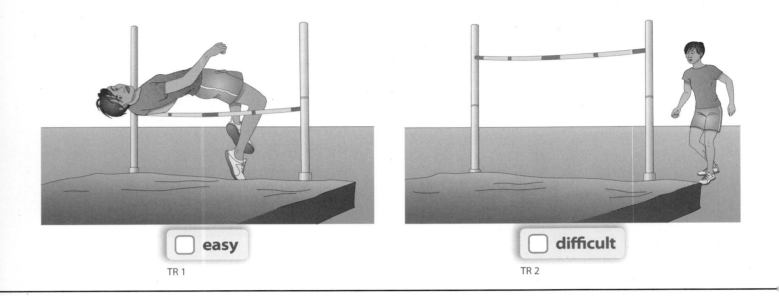

☐ **easy**

TR 1

☐ **difficult**

TR 2

Check Your Understanding

A. Complete the paragraph with the correct word from the word bank.

easy	difficult	impossible	problem

Running seems to be very (1) _____. All you have to do is put one foot in front of the other and go, right? So when my cousin asked me to run a marathon with her, I didn't think it would be a (2) _____. All I would have to do is run and run, for 26.2 miles. However, when I started preparing for the marathon, I realized how (3) _____ it would be. I got tired after a few miles. As the day of the race came near, I realized that I simply could not do it. It was (4) _____ for me to run the whole marathon at that time. I plan to keep training and try again soon.

□ problem
TR 3

□ impossible
TR 4

Definitions

Something that is **difficult** is not easy to do, understand, or deal with.

When a task is **easy**, you can do it without difficulty.

Something that is **impossible** cannot be done or cannot happen.

A **problem** is something or someone that causes difficulties, or that makes you worry.

B. Circle the best example of each word.

1. easy

   a. 1 + 1

   b. $2(x - 17)^2 \div \pi \times 14$

2. difficult

   a. walking down the street

   b. climbing up a mountain

3. impossible

   a. flying to school, like a bird

   b. taking the bus to school

4. problem

   a. having fun with your best friend

   b. having a fight with your best friend

Challenge Words

Check (✔) the words you already know.

□ cinch   □ difficulty   □ fluent   □ hardship   □ unbearable

□ convenient   □ ease   □ grueling   □ simplify   □ uneasy

240. Safety and Danger

Check (✔) the words you already know. Then, listen and repeat.

Tracks 1–6

☐ **danger**

TR 1

☐ **trouble**

TR 2

☐ **risk**

TR 3

Check Your Understanding

A. Choose the sentence that correctly uses the underlined word.

1. a. It is <u>safe</u> to ride your bicycle without a helmet on.

   b. It is <u>safe</u> to ride your bicycle with a helmet on.

2. a. When you are asleep in your bed at night, you are probably in <u>danger</u>.

   b. When you are lost in the woods at night, you are probably in <u>danger</u>.

3. a. It might be <u>dangerous</u> to walk down a dark city street alone late at night.

   b. It is very <u>dangerous</u> to walk in the library alone.

4. a. If you go on a hike without a map, you take a <u>risk</u> that you will get lost.

   b. If you go to the beach, you take a <u>risk</u> that you will have fun.

5. a. I know this area very well, so I should have <u>trouble</u> finding your apartment.

   b. I was late to work because I had <u>trouble</u> with my car.

6. a. It is <u>unsafe</u> to go to science class.

   b. It is <u>unsafe</u> to do a science experiment without goggles to protect your eyes.

- ☐ **dangerous**
- ☐ **unsafe**

TR 4 and TR 5

- ☐ **safe**

TR 6

Definitions

Danger is a situation when something unpleasant happens, or a situation where you may be harmed or killed.

When something is **dangerous**, it may harm you.

A **risk** is an action that might cause injury or harm.

Something that is **safe** is not dangerous and will not cause any harm.

Trouble is a problem or a difficulty.

When something is **unsafe**, it is dangerous.

B. Write **T** for **true statements** and **F** for **false statements**.

1. _____ It is safe to touch a hot stove.

2. _____ If you think that there is danger at your house, you should call the police.

3. _____ It is dangerous to go in the ocean if you do not know how to swim.

4. _____ If you take a risk, you will definitely have good results.

5. _____ When there is trouble with your car, there is a problem with it.

6. _____ It is unsafe to wear your seatbelt in the car.

Challenge Words

Check (✔) the words you already know.

- ☐ harmful
- ☐ harmless
- ☐ hazard
- ☐ immune
- ☐ jeopardy
- ☐ peril
- ☐ pitfall
- ☐ protective
- ☐ secure
- ☐ treacherous

68. Students and Teachers

Check (✔) the words you already know. Then, listen and repeat.

Tracks 1–6

☐ **graduate**

TR 1

☐ **principal**

TR 2

PRINCIPAL JONES

Check Your Understanding

A. Circle the correct description of each word.

1. principal

    a. somebody who is in charge of a school

    b. somebody who works in the cafeteria of a school

2. student

    a. somebody who gives new information to others

    b. somebody who learns new information from others

3. teacher

    a. somebody who gives new information to others

    b. somebody who learns new information from others

4. graduate

    a. somebody who finishes her studies

    b. somebody who begins her studies

5. pupil

    a. a student who is an adult

    b. a student who is a child

6. schoolteacher

    a. a teacher who teaches science, language, or math

    b. a teacher who teaches yoga, dance, or cooking

schoolteacher
teacher

TR 3 and TR 4

pupil
student

TR 5 and TR 6

Definitions

A **graduate** is a student who has completed a course at a high school, college, or university.

The **principal** of a school is the person in charge of the school.

A **pupil** is a child who attends an elementary school.

A **schoolteacher** is a teacher in a school.

A **student** is a person who is studying at a school, college, or university.

A **teacher** is a person whose job is to give lessons at a school or a college.

B. Underline the correct word to complete each sentence.

1. A (**pupil / schoolteacher**) from Mrs. Manning's fourth-grade class won the contest.

2. Charles is a (**principal / graduate**) of the state university, and now he works as an engineer.

3. Alicia got called to the (**principal's / schoolteacher's**) office after she was very late to class.

4. Who is your favorite (**pupil / teacher**)—Mr. Alvarez or Mrs. Bennett?

5. There are only twelve (**principals / students**) in my art class.

6. This college has a good program to prepare students to become (**pupils / schoolteachers**).

Challenge Words

Check (✔) the words you already know.

☐ adviser	☐ dean	☐ instructor	☐ professor	☐ tutor
☐ counselor	☐ freshman	☐ mentor	☐ sophomore	

88. Medical Occupations

Check (✔) the words you already know. Then, listen and repeat.

 Tracks 1–3

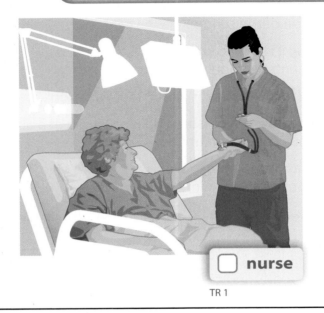

☐ **nurse**

TR 1

☐ **doctor**

TR 2

Check Your Understanding

A. Circle the name of the person to go to in each situation.

1. You need to get weighed and measured before your physical examination.

   a. dentist   b. doctor   c. nurse

2. You just got x-rays of your back, and want to know the results.

   a. dentist   b. doctor   c. nurse

3. One of your teeth hurts.

   a. dentist   b. doctor   c. nurse

4. You are in the hospital and need help getting out of bed.

   a. dentist   b. doctor   c. nurse

5. It is time to have your teeth cleaned.

   a. dentist   b. doctor   c. nurse

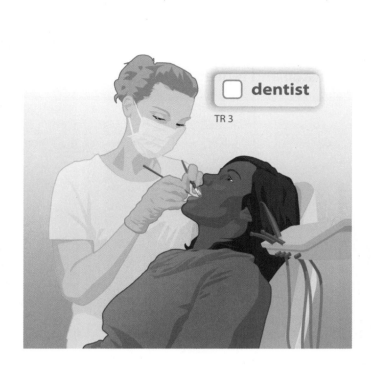

☐ dentist

TR 3

Definitions

A **dentist** is a person whose job is to examine and treat people's teeth.

A **doctor** is a person whose job is to treat people who are sick or injured.

A **nurse** is a person whose job is to care for people who are sick.

B. Choose the correct word from the word bank to complete each sentence.

dentist	doctor	nurse

1. Marie hates going to the _____ , especially if she needs a filling in one of her teeth.

2. Martin works as a _____ in a doctor's office.

3. Andrew finally became a _____ after eight years of medical school.

Challenge Words

Check (✔) the words you already know.

☐ dentistry   ☐ intern   ☐ physician   ☐ surgeon   ☐ therapist

146. Actions Related to Work

Check (✔) the words you already know. Then, listen and repeat.

Tracks 1–4

☐ **hire**

TR 1

☐ **work**

TR 2

☐ **labor**

TR 3

Check Your Understanding

A. Choose the correct word from the word bank to complete each sentence.

quit	work	hire	labor

1. The interview went well, so I hope they _____ me for the job.

2. To build the long brick wall, the worker had to _____ for many hours.

3. Does Michael _____ in an office downtown now?

4. I decided to _____ my last job because this one pays more.

John's Cafe

☐ **quit**

TR 4

Definitions

To **hire** someone means to pay them to do a job for you.

To **labor** over something means to work very hard at it.

To **quit** means to choose to stop doing a job.

To **work** means to have a job and earn money for it.

B. Match each word to the correct description. One description will not be used.

1. _____ quit
2. _____ work
3. _____ hire
4. _____ labor

a. to give someone a job to do for pay

b. to work very hard

c. to try to complete a job

d. to stop working at a job

e. to have a job

Challenge Words

Check (✔) the words you already know.

☐ drudge   ☐ employ   ☐ retire   ☐ toil

☐ effort   ☐ engage   ☐ strive   ☐ travail

167. Performers and Entertainers

Check (✔) the words you already know. Then, listen and repeat.

Tracks 1–6

☐ dancer

TR 1

☐ model

TR 2

☐ magician

TR 3

Check Your Understanding

A. Write **T** for **true statements** and **F** for **false statements**.

1. _____ A magician shows off new fashions so that people can take pictures of him.

2. _____ You might find a clown at a birthday party, at a fair, or at a circus.

3. _____ An actress is a female who plays parts in movies, plays, and television shows.

4. _____ A dancer dresses up in funny clothing to make people laugh.

5. _____ Actors only perform in movies.

6. _____ People take photos of models.

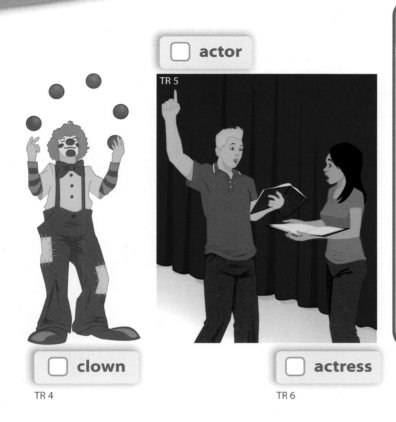

actor

clown

TR 4

actress

TR 6

Definitions

An **actor** is a man whose job is acting in plays, television shows, or movies.

An **actress** is a woman whose job is acting in plays, television shows, or movies.

A **clown** is a performer who wears funny clothes and makeup and does silly things to make people laugh.

A **dancer** is a person who moves his or her body along with music.

A **magician** is a person who entertains people by doing magic tricks.

A **model** is a person who poses for artists, photographers, or with products for sale.

B. Underline the correct word to complete each sentence.

1. Anna trained for years to be a (**dancer** / **clown**), and now she performs in the ballet.

2. I have seen this (**actor** / **actress**) in another movie, and she was horrible.

3. Claire is a (**magician** / **model**) who travels for work and gets to wear great clothes.

4. The (**clown** / **model**) wore a large red nose and white makeup on his face.

5. Hundreds of (**clowns** / **actors**) are going to try out for a part in the movie.

6. Uncle Jim is a (**magician** / **model**) and always does tricks to entertain everyone.

Challenge Words

Check (✔) the words you already know.

- comic
- performer
- ventriloquist

173. Royalty and Statesmen

Check (✔) the words you already know. Then, listen and repeat.

Tracks 1–9

☐ **mayor**

TR 1

☐ **candidate**

TR 2

☐ **president**

TR 3

☐ **official**

TR 4

Check Your Understanding

A. Circle the correct word to complete each sentence.

1. Government _____ are saying that they may have to raise taxes next year.
   a. officials   b. queens   c. princesses

2. The _____ was only fifteen when she began to rule her country.
   a. prince   b. queen   c. candidate

3. Every four years, the city holds elections for a new _____.
   a. knight   b. mayor   c. king

4. There are six _____ who want to become governor.
   a. kings   b. presidents   c. candidates

5. Because he is the youngest son, the _____ may never become _____.
   a. queen / king   b. prince / king   c. king / princess

6. Lisa looked like a _____ in the beautiful pink gown.
   a. princess   b. president   c. king

7. The _____ wore a long robe and a heavy crown at special events.
   a. president   b. king   c. candidate

8. It must have been difficult for _____ to wear such heavy metal armor and ride on horses.
   a. candidates   b. princes   c. knights

9. The _____ of the United States travels in his own special airplane.
   a. queen   b. president   c. princess

☐ queen	☐ king
TR 5	TR 6

☐ knight	☐ prince	☐ princess
TR 7	TR 8	TR 9

Definitions

A **candidate** is someone who is trying to get a particular job or trying to win a political position.

A **king** is a man from a royal family, who is the head of state or the ruler of a country.

In the past, a **knight** was a special type of soldier who rode a horse.

The **mayor** of a city or a town is the person who is responsible for its government.

An **official** is a person who holds a position of power in an organization.

The **president** is the head of the government in some countries.

A **prince** is a male member of a royal family, especially the son of the king or queen or the husband of a princess.

A **princess** is a female member of a royal family, especially the daughter of a king or queen or the wife of a prince.

A **queen** is a woman from a royal family, who is the head of state or the ruler of a country.

B. Underline the correct word to complete each sentence.

1. Modern soldiers still wear protective clothing, but they no longer dress like (**kings / knights**).

2. In the United States, there is no (**queen / candidate**). The wife of the president is called the First Lady.

3. School (**princesses / officials**) cancelled classes yesterday due to the snow.

4. The (**knight / mayor**) and the police chief will be speaking at City Hall today.

5. In the story, the (**knight / princess**) kisses a frog, and it turns into a handsome prince.

6. Richard Smith is the best (**king / candidate**) for mayor because he has the most experience.

7. Who was the forty-second (**king / president**) of the United States?

8. The (**prince / king**) is married to a beautiful princess.

9. When George III was the (**official / king**) of England, America rebelled against him.

Challenge Words

Check (✔) the words you already know.

☐ ambassador   ☐ congressman   ☐ dictator   ☐ monarch   ☐ senator

☐ chief   ☐ congresswoman   ☐ diplomat   ☐ politician   ☐ vice president

229. Names of People in Sports

Check (✔) the words you already know. Then, listen and repeat.

Tracks 1–8

☐ **loser**
TR 3

☐ **winner**
TR 4

☐ **batter**
TR 1

☐ **coach**
TR 2

☐ **athlete**
TR 5

Check Your Understanding

A. Choose the correct word from the word bank to complete each sentence.

athletes	boxers	coach	runner
batter	catcher	losers	winner

1. Lynn is a long-distance _____. She runs at least ten miles each day.

2. All the players gathered around the _____ to see what he wanted them to do next.

3. The _____ of the tennis game will win a big trophy.

4. Many _____ train by punching a leather bag that hangs from the ceiling.

5. Most professional _____ make a lot of money to play their sport.

6. The _____ hit the ball over the fence for a homerun.

7. The _____ were disappointed, but they congratulated the other team.

8. The _____ on a baseball team protects his face with a mask.

catcher

TR 6

runner

TR 7

boxer

TR 8

Definitions

An **athlete** is a person who is good at any type of physical sports, exercise, or games.

In some sports, a **batter** is a person who hits the ball.

A **boxer** is a person who fights with fists or boxing gloves according to the rules of boxing.

In baseball, the **catcher** is the player who stands behind the batter and catches the balls thrown by the pitcher.

A **coach** is someone who is in charge of teaching and managing a person or a sports team.

The **loser** of a game or race is the person who does not win.

A **runner** is a person who runs, or who is running.

The **winner** of a prize, a race, or a competition is the one that wins it.

B. Underline the correct word to complete each sentence.

1. The baseball went right by the (**catcher / boxer**) and into the crowd.

2. The (**athlete / coach**) told the players that they would not be allowed to play if their grades fell.

3. Nobody likes to be the (**winner / loser**) of a game.

4. The (**runner / boxer**) punched his opponent under his chin to knock him out.

5. The (**catcher / batter**) swung at the ball but did not hit it.

6. The person who can stand on one foot the longest will be the (**coach / winner**) of the contest.

7. In college, (**losers / athletes**) have to keep up their grades if they want to play sports.

8. The (**catcher / runner**) finished the foot race in less than five minutes.

Challenge Words

Check (✔) the words you already know.

- [ ] acrobat
- [ ] daredevil
- [ ] jockey
- [ ] lifeguard
- [ ] player
- [ ] referee
- [ ] timekeeper
- [ ] trainer
- [ ] umpire
- [ ] underdog

236. Occupations (General)

Check (✔) the words you already know. Then, listen and repeat.

Tracks 1–7

☐ **career**

TR 1

☐ **chore**

TR 2

☐ **worker**

TR 4

☐ **job**

TR 3

Check Your Understanding

A. Circle the best example of each word.

1. job
   - a. doing math homework
   - b. stocking shelves at a supermarket

2. career
   - a. working as a lawyer
   - b. painting your bedroom

3. chore
   - a. washing a car
   - b. buying a new car

4. housework
   - a. working in a clothing store
   - b. folding clean clothing

5. profession
   - a. working as a babysitter
   - b. working as a dentist

6. task
   - a. writing the answers to your homework questions
   - b. asking your teacher a question about your homework

7. worker
   - a. a person who tells people what work to do
   - b. a person who does the work that somebody gives him

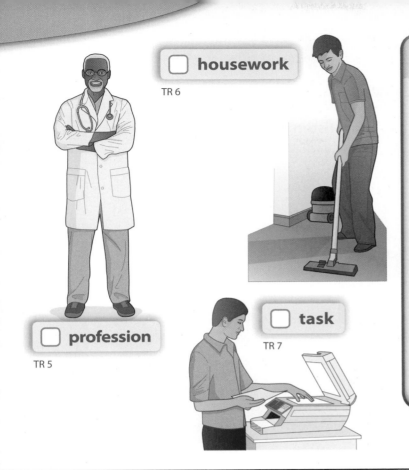

housework

TR 6

profession

TR 5

task

TR 7

Definitions

A **career** is a job, or the years of your life that you spend working.

A **chore** is a job that you have to do, for example, taking out the garbage.

A **job** is work that someone does to earn money.

Housework is work that you do to keep a house clean and neat.

A **profession** is a type of job for which you need special education or training, such as a doctor.

A **task** is a piece of work that you have to do.

A **worker** is a person who works, who is below the level of a manager.

B. Underline the correct word to complete each sentence.

1. All the (**workers** / **professions**) in the factory took an hour break for lunch.

2. Patty's (**housework** / **job**) is to prepare students to become nurses.

3. Working in the medical (**profession** / **chore**) generally requires a lot of training.

4. Chris has several small (**careers** / **tasks**) to do before he can leave work.

5. My parents do not give me too many (**workers** / **chores**), but I help with the dishes and take out the trash.

6. Cindy hired somebody to help with the (**profession** / **housework**) because she was so busy at her job.

7. Jermaine is studying for a (**career** / **task**) as a lawyer.

Challenge Words

Check (✔) the words you already know.

- [ ] craft
- [ ] errand
- [ ] livelihood
- [ ] occupation
- [ ] production
- [ ] profession
- [ ] role
- [ ] sideline
- [ ] vocation

197

257. Domains of Work

Check (✔) the words you already know. Then, listen and repeat.

Tracks 1–7

☐ business

TR 1

☐ military

TR 2

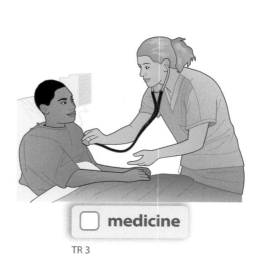

☐ medicine

TR 3

Check Your Understanding

A. Match each word to the correct description. One description will not be used.

1. _____ business   a. the study of natural things such as chemistry

2. _____ law   b. the armed forces

3. _____ medicine   c. the field of work in which people grow food

4. _____ military   d. the field of work in which people sell products or services

5. _____ religion   e. the field of work in which people treat illness or injuries

6. _____ science   f. the use of science to make life easier for people

7. _____ technology   g. the system of rules established by the government

                                              h. a system of beliefs in a god or gods

Definitions

Business is work that is related to producing, buying, and selling things.

The **law** is a system of rules that a society or a government develops to deal with things like crime.

Medicine is the treatment of illness and injuries performed by doctors and nurses.

The **military** are the armed forces (army, navy, air force) of a country.

A **religion** is a particular system of beliefs in a god or gods and the activities that are connected with this system.

Science is the study of natural things such as biology, chemistry, or physics.

Technology is any system or device that is the result of scientific knowledge and is most often used to help make jobs easier.

☐ law
TR 4

☐ science
TR 5

☐ technology
TR 6

☐ religion
TR 7

B. Write **T** for **true statements** and **F** for **false statements**.

1. _____ The law is a system of rules in a country.

2. _____ Studying plants is a science.

3. _____ A police officer is an example of someone who works in medicine.

4. _____ A person who works in the military is part of the armed forces of a country.

5. _____ People who work in religion often work in places of worship.

6. _____ If you use a computer or a smart phone, you are using technology.

7. _____ Somebody who works in business probably does not care about making money.

Challenge Words

Check (✔) the words you already know.

☐ agriculture ☐ industry ☐ politics

264. Artists and Performers

Check (✔) the words you already know. Then, listen and repeat.

Tracks 1–5

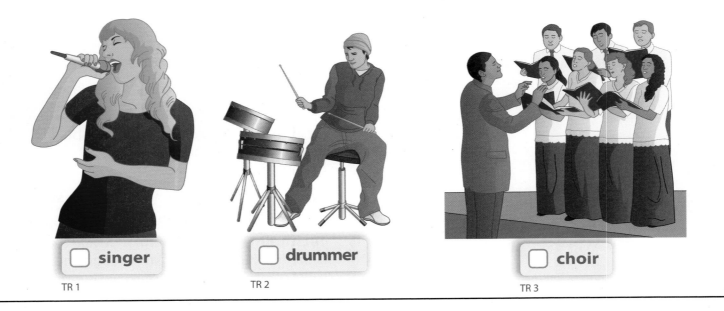

☐ **singer**

TR 1

☐ **drummer**

TR 2

☐ **choir**

TR 3

Check Your Understanding

A. Match each word to the correct description. One description will not be used.

1. _____ artist
2. _____ choir
3. _____ drummer
4. _____ painter
5. _____ singer

a. a person who makes music with his or her voice

b. a person who creates pictures with a camera

c. a person who creates any kind of art

d. a group of people who sing together

e. a person who uses sticks to play an instrument

f. a person who creates pictures with paint

☐ artist

TR 4

☐ painter

TR 5

Definitions

An **artist** is someone who draws, paints, or creates works of art.

A **choir** is a group of people who sing together.

A **drummer** is a person who plays the drums, a simple musical instrument that you hit with sticks or with your hands.

A **painter** is an artist who paints pictures.

A **singer** is a person who sings.

B. Underline the correct word to complete each sentence.

1. Veronica is not a famous (**artist / drummer**), but some of her work is in the local museum.

2. The (**choir / painter**) will be singing at the holiday concert.

3. The (**choir / drummer**) keeps the beat while the rest of the band plays.

4. The (**singer / drummer**) of this song has a beautiful voice.

5. This (**painter / choir**) used interesting colors and shapes in his picture.

Challenge Words

Check (✔) the words you already know.

☐ conductor   ☐ musician   ☐ soprano
☐ designer   ☐ photographer   ☐ violinist

265. Public Officials

Check (✔) the words you already know. Then, listen and repeat.

Tracks 1–5

☐ **firefighter**

TR 1

☐ **officer**

TR 2

☐ **soldier**

TR 3

Check Your Understanding

A. Circle the correct word to complete each sentence.

1. Jon called the county _____ office when his car was stolen.

   a. soldier's   b. firefighter's   c. sheriff's

2. As soon as you smell smoke, you should contact _____ .

   a. police officers   b. firefighters   c. soldiers

3. After working on the ship for several years, Michael became _____ on the ship.

   a. a firefighter   b. a sheriff   c. an officer

4. By the time the _____ arrived, the robber had already left.

   a. police officer   b. firefighter   c. soldier

5. Even when there are no wars, a _____ still has a job to do.

   a. police officer   b. sheriff   c. soldier

sheriff

TR 4

police officer

TR 5

Definitions

A **firefighter** is a person whose job is to put out fires.

In the armed forces, such as the army or navy, an **officer** is a person who is in charge of other people.

A **police officer** is a person who is a member of the police force.

In the United States, a **sheriff** is a law enforcement officer. A **sheriff** is usually responsible for a county or a region.

A **soldier** is a member of an army.

B. Write **T** for **true statements** and **F** for **false statements**.

1. _____ A sheriff is a leader in the armed forces.

2. _____ Officers are people who put out fires.

3. _____ If you think that someone is trying to break into your house, you should call a police officer.

4. _____ A soldier is a member of the police force.

5. _____ A firefighter must wear special clothing as protection from fire.

Challenge Words

Check (✔) the words you already know.

- [ ] admiral
- [ ] captain
- [ ] colonel
- [ ] corporal
- [ ] deputy
- [ ] detective
- [ ] lieutenant
- [ ] marshal
- [ ] sergeant
- [ ] trooper

266. Religious and Clergy

Check (✔) the words you already know. Then, listen and repeat.

Tracks 1–5

☐ **pastor**

TR 1

☐ **pope**

TR 2

☐ **nun**

TR 3

Check Your Understanding

A. Write **T** for **true statements** and **F** for **false statements**.

1. _____ A priest can perform religious ceremonies.

2. _____ A nun is a man who prays in a special building with other men.

3. _____ A minister leads a church service.

4. _____ The pope is a regular priest in the Roman Catholic Church.

5. _____ A pastor is responsible for running a church.

B. Circle the correct description for each word.

1. minister

   a. a leader in the church who might perform different jobs

   b. a person in the church who cleans up after each mass

2. nun

   a. a woman who is religious and prays with her family

   b. a woman who is religious and sometimes lives with other religious women

☐ **priest**

TR 4

☐ **minister**

TR 5

3. pastor

   a. a leader of a church

   b. a person who goes to church

4. pope

   a. the leader of the Roman Catholic Church

   b. the leader of the Orthodox Jewish faith

5. priest

   a. a person who heads the church

   b. a person who works in a church

Challenge Words

Check (✔) the words you already know.

☐ apostle   ☐ cardinal   ☐ deacon   ☐ missionary   ☐ prophet

☐ bishop   ☐ clergyman   ☐ hermit   ☐ monk   ☐ rabbi

297. Small Businesses

Check (✔) the words you already know. Then, listen and repeat.

 Tracks 1–3

 ☐ **butcher**

TR 1

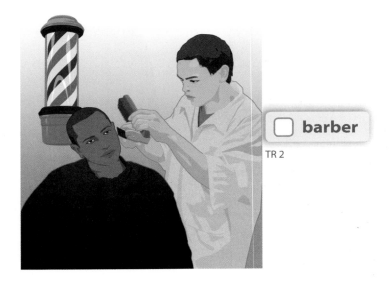 ☐ **barber**

TR 2

Check Your Understanding

A. Circle the name of the person to go to in each situation.

1. It is your sister's birthday and you need a cake.

   a. baker   b. butcher   c. barber

2. You wish to make hamburgers for your friends.

   a. baker   b. butcher   c. barber

3. You are taking your little brother to get his hair cut.

   a. baker   b. butcher   c. barber

4. You want to buy sausages.

   a. baker   b. butcher   c. barber

5. Your mother asked you to buy bread for dinner.

   a. baker   b. butcher   c. barber

☐ baker

TR 3

B. Choose the correct word from the word bank to complete each sentence.

baker	barber	butcher

1. The _____ wrapped up several slices of meat and two sausages for us.

2. Do you know if the _____ is working today? I need a haircut.

3. Annette is a fabulous _____ who makes delicious chocolate-chip cookies.

Challenge Words

Check (✔) the words you already know.

☐ blacksmith   ☐ florist   ☐ smith

☐ bodyguard   ☐ miller   ☐ tailor

333. Writers and Reporters

Check (✔) the words you already know. Then, listen and repeat.

🎧 Tracks 1–3

□ writer

TR 1

□ author

TR 2

Check Your Understanding

A. Write **T** for **true statements** and **F** for **false statements**.

1. _____ You might have a speaker come into your school to talk about a topic.

2. _____ An author needs to have great skill at public speaking.

3. _____ People can work as writers for magazines and television shows.

4. _____ A writer only writes books.

speaker

TR 3

B. Underline the correct word to complete each sentence.

1. The (**author / speaker**) kept everyone's attention throughout the presentation.

2. Jenny works as a (**writer / speaker**) for a famous magazine.

3. I have several novels by this (**author / speaker**). I love the way she writes.

Challenge Words

Check (✔) the words you already know.

☐ critic   ☐ narrator   ☐ publisher   ☐ scribe   ☐ weatherman

☐ editor   ☐ poet   ☐ reporter   ☐ spokesperson

334. People Who Clean Up

Check (✔) the words you already know. Then, listen and repeat.

Tracks 1–3

☐ **custodian**

TR 1

☐ **janitor**

TR 2

Check Your Understanding

A. Circle the correct answer.

1. Whose job is it to take trash away in a large truck?

    a. garbage man   b. janitor   c. custodian

2. Whose job is it to repair the heater in an office building?

    a. garbage man   b. janitor   c. custodian

3. Whose job is it to wash the floors at a school?

    a. garbage man   b. janitor   c. custodian

4. Who might work to clean an office building at night?

    a. garbage man   b. janitor   c. custodian

garbage man

TR 3

Definitions

The **custodian** of a building is the person whose job is to make repairs and take care of the building and the grounds around it.

A **garbage man** is a person whose job is to take people's garbage away.

A **janitor** is a person whose job is to clean and take care of a building.

B. Match each word to the correct description. One description will not be used.

1. _____ garbage man

2. _____ janitor

3. _____ custodian

a. the person who cleans the classrooms at your school

b. the person who cooks and serves the food at your school

c. the person who takes your trash away in a large truck

d. the person who takes care of your school grounds

355. Assistants and Supervisors

Check (✔) the words you already know. Then, listen and repeat.

Tracks 1–3

☐ **boss**

TR 1

☐ **leader**

TR 2

Check Your Understanding

A. Match each word to the correct description. One description will not be used.

1. _____ boss
2. _____ leader
3. _____ owner

a. the person who runs his or her own business

b. the person who gives you directions on what to do at work

c. the person who owns the apartment or house you live in

d. the person who is in charge of a group

FLOWERS

☐ **owner**

TR 3

Definitions

Your **boss** is the person in charge of you at the place where you work.

The **leader** of a group of people or an organization is the person who is in charge.

When you are the **owner** of a business, it belongs to you.

B. Choose the correct word from the word bank to complete each sentence.

boss	leader	owners

1. Unfortunately, my _____ will not let me have Friday night off.

2. Michelle and Tim are the _____ of the new coffee shop on the corner.

3. This company wants to hire someone who is a good _____ for the company.

Challenge Words

Check (✔) the words you already know.

☐ apprentice   ☐ chairman   ☐ foreman   ☐ landlord   ☐ superintendent

☐ assistant   ☐ director   ☐ landlady   ☐ manager   ☐ supervisor

356. Occupations Usually Held by Youth

Check (✔) the words you already know. Then, listen and repeat.

Tracks 1–2

☐ babysitter

TR 1

☐ paperboy

TR 2

Definitions

A **babysitter** is a person who takes care of a child when the child's parents are not at home.

A **paperboy** is someone who delivers newspapers to people's homes.

Check Your Understanding

A. Choose the correct word from the word bank to complete each sentence. Each word will be used twice.

babysitter	paperboy

1. Our _____ Tommy always delivers the newspaper early in the morning.

2. The Millers asked the _____ to take care of Jake while they went out.

3. When Tania is old enough, she will be a good _____ because she is great with children.

4. Pedro has to finish his duties as a _____ before he goes to school.

B. Circle the name of the person that matches each situation.

1. A couple has tickets to a concert but cannot take their son.

   a. babysitter   b. paperboy

2. The newsstand down the street has closed, but you still want the daily news.

   a. babysitter   b. paperboy

3. A father has to work an extra day this week and cannot leave his daughter home alone.

   a. babysitter   b. paperboy

357. Discoverers and Scientists

Check (✔) the words you already know. Then, listen and repeat.

Tracks 1–3

Definitions

An **astronaut** is a person who is trained for traveling in space.

Geography is the study of the earth's surface, its features, its climate, and its people.

A **scientist** is someone whose job is to teach or do research in science.

☐ **scientist**

TR 1

☐ **astronaut**

TR 2

☐ **geography**

TR 3

Check Your Understanding

A. Choose the sentence that correctly uses the underlined word.

1. a. Elizabeth would like to be an <u>astronaut</u>, so she is studying books about animals.

    b. Elizabeth would like to be an <u>astronaut</u>, so she is studying books about space.

2. a. George is working on his multiplication tables to prepare for his <u>geography</u> test.

    b. George is studying maps of the earth's surface to prepare for his <u>geography</u> test.

3. a. Thousands of <u>scientists</u> are working to find a cure for this disease.

    b. Thousands of <u>scientists</u> are working to create new textbooks.

B. Match each word to the group of words they are related to. One group will not be used.

1. _____ astronaut

2. _____ geography

3. _____ scientist

    a. laboratory, tests, white coat and gloves

    b. outer space, travel, explore

    c. maps, globe, land forms

    d. rocks, metals, soil

Challenge Words

Check (✔) the words you already know.

☐ astronomy ☐ chemistry ☐ economics ☐ inventor ☐ researcher

☐ biology ☐ ecology ☐ geology ☐ psychology ☐ veterinarian

358. Occupations Associated with Imprisonment / Slavery

Check (✔) the words you already know. Then, listen and repeat.

Tracks 1–3

Definitions

A **guard** is a person whose job is to guard a particular place or person.

A **prisoner** is a person who is not free, usually because they are in prison.

A **slave** is someone who belongs to another person and is forced to work for that person for little or no money.

☐ prisoner
TR 2

☐ guard
TR 1

☐ slave
TR 3

Check Your Understanding

A. Match each word to the correct description. One description will not be used.

1. _____ guard   a. a person who is forced to work for little or no pay

2. _____ prisoner   b. a person in ancient Rome who fought as entertainment

3. _____ slave   c. a person who watches prisoners

                        d. a person who is in jail for committing a crime

B. Choose the correct word from the word bank to complete each sentence.

guard	prisoners	slaves

1. _____ worked on farms from morning to night, without pay or time off.

2. The _____ let the woman through the prison gates so that she could visit her son.

3. The _____ leave their cells twice a day for meals in the main hall.

Challenge Words

Check (✔) the words you already know.

☐ gladiator   ☐ warden

359. Construction and Repairmen

Check (✔) the words you already know. Then, listen and repeat.

Tracks 1–2

☐ **plumber**

TR 1

☐ **repairman**

TR 2

Definitions

A **plumber** is a person whose job is to put in and repair water pipes, drains, and other kitchen and bathroom fixtures.

A **repairman** is a person whose job is to fix broken machines, such as refrigerators and stoves.

Check Your Understanding

A. Circle the name of the person that matches each situation.

1. Water from your toilet is going all over the bathroom floor.   a. plumber   b. repairman
2. The refrigerator is not keeping your food cold.   a. plumber   b. repairman
3. Your computer keeps giving you an error message.   a. plumber   b. repairman
4. You want a new sink in your kitchen.   a. plumber   b. repairman
5. Your television will not switch channels.   a. plumber   b. repairman

B. Circle the things that a **plumber** can fix. Underline the things that a **repairman** can fix.

stove	toilet
shower	sink
refrigerator	water pipes
furnace	dryer

Challenge Words

Check (✔) the words you already know.

☐ carpenter   ☐ draftsman   ☐ mason   ☐ mechanic

360. Legal Professions

Check (✔) the words you already know. Then, listen and repeat.

Tracks 1–2

☐ **lawyer**   ☐ **judge**

TR 1   TR 2

Definitions

A **judge** is the person in a court of law who decides how criminals should be punished.

A **lawyer** is a person who advises people about the law and represents them in court.

Check Your Understanding

A. Write **T** for **true statements** and **F** for **false statements**.

1. _____ A judge's job is to advise people in court so that they stay out of trouble.

2. _____ It is important for lawyers and judges to know the law.

3. _____ Lawyers only work in the courts.

4. _____ If a person gets in trouble with the law, a judge might decide his punishment.

B. Underline the correct word to complete each sentence.

1. The (**judge / lawyer**) had to decide if the man should go to jail, or if he should be allowed to go free.

2. Keith asked the (**judge / lawyer**) to represent him in court next week.

3. The criminal was found guilty, and the (**judge / lawyer**) decided that he would spend six years in prison.

4. Melanie is studying to be a (**judge / lawyer**). She wants to give legal advice to big companies.

Challenge Words

Check (✔) the words you already know.

☐ attorney   ☐ counselor

361. Servants

Check (✔) the words you already know. Then, listen and repeat.

Tracks 1–2

☐ **maid**

TR 1

☐ **servant**

TR 2

Definitions

A **maid** is a woman whose job is to clean rooms in a hotel or in a private house.

A **servant** is someone who works at another person's home, doing work such as cooking, serving food, or cleaning.

Check Your Understanding

A. Circle **maid** or **servant** for each statement. If both words apply, circle both of them.

maid	servant	1. can be male or female
maid	servant	2. works in a hotel
maid	servant	3. a person who cleans
maid	servant	4. helps with cooking

B. Choose the correct word from the box to complete each sentence. Each word will be used twice.

> servants   maids

1. The hotel has 300 rooms and only 10 _____ .

2. The Johnson family has four _____ : two cooks, a gardener, and a nanny.

3. Every morning, the _____ make all the beds at the inn.

4. One hundred years ago, many people had _____ , but these days only the very rich do.

Challenge Words

Check (✔) the words you already know.

☐ butler   ☐ chauffeur   ☐ doorman   ☐ housekeeper   ☐ usher

392. Food Service Occupations

Check (✔) the words you already know. Then, listen and repeat

Tracks 1–2

Definitions

A **waiter** is a man whose job is to take orders and serve food in a restaurant.

A **waitress** is a woman whose job is to take orders and serve food in a restaurant.

☐ **waiter**

TR 1

☐ **waitress**

TR 2

Check Your Understanding

A. Complete each sentence with the word **waiter** or **waitress**.

1. Our _____ was great, so we should leave him a big tip.

2. Please get our _____. She is the blonde girl by the door.

3. Jane's daughter is working as a _____ while she goes to college.

4. The new restaurant is looking for employees. Jim is applying
   to be a _____.

B. Choose the sentence that correctly uses the underlined word or words.

1. a. Our <u>waiter</u> cooked the hamburger perfectly.

   b. Our <u>waiter</u> brought us the check at the end of the meal.

2. a. The <u>waitress</u> dropped a tray of drinks on her way to a table.

   b. The <u>waitress</u> sat at the table while the customer served her.

3. a. The restaurant is hiring new <u>waiters and waitresses</u>.

   b. The hospital is hiring new <u>waiters and waitresses</u>.

Challenge Words

Check (✔) the words you already know.

☐ busboy   ☐ chef   ☐ dishwasher

393. Messengers

Check (✔) the word if you already know it. Then, listen and repeat.

Track 1

☐ **mailman**

TR 1

Definition

A **mailman** is a person whose job is to collect and deliver letters and packages that you send by mail.

Check Your Understanding

A. Check (✔) the things that a **mailman** might bring to your house.

☐ package

☐ lunch

☐ homework

☐ magazine

☐ letter

☐ bus

B. Write **T** for **true statements** and **F** for **false statements**.

1. _____ A mailman usually carries his mail in a bag.

2. _____ You might give your letters to a mailman who will take them to the post office.

3. _____ Your mailman takes your mail directly to the person you are sending it to.

4. _____ The mailman comes to your house in the middle of the night.

Challenge Words

Check (✔) the words you already know.

☐ courier   ☐ postmaster

394. Occupations Associated with the Outdoors

Check (✔) the word if you already know it. Then, listen and repeat.

Track 1

☐ **cowboy**

TR 1

Definition

A **cowboy** is a man who rides a horse and takes care of cows or cattle in North America.

Check Your Understanding

A. Write **T** for **true statements** and **F** for **false statements**.

1. _____ A cowboy usually wears a large hat.

2. _____ A cowboy works in an office.

3. _____ A cowboy works only with horses.

4. _____ To be a cowboy, you need to know how to ride a horse.

B. Circle the correct answer.

1. Which of the following would a cowboy wear to work?

   a. boots, jeans, and a large hat   b. a suit and a tie

2. Where does a cowboy work?

   a. in an office in the city   b. on a large, open area of land

3. How does a cowboy move around at work?

   a. in an airplane   b. on horseback

4. Where are cowboys more likely to be found?

   a. in the United States   b. in China

Challenge Words

Check (✔) the words you already know

☐ cavalry   ☐ cowhand   ☐ hunter   ☐ miner   ☐ rancher

☐ cowgirl   ☐ deckhand   ☐ lumberjack   ☐ prospector   ☐ shepherd

395. People Who Buy and Sell

Check (✔) the word if you already know it. Then, listen and repeat.

Track 1

☐ **customer**

TR 1

Definition

A **customer** is someone who buys an item from another person or a business.

Check Your Understanding

A. Write **T** for **true statements** and **F** for **false statements**.

1. _____ A customer is somebody who sells things to other people.

2. _____ If you buy a DVD at a store, you are a customer of that store.

3. _____ You are a customer when you visit your friend's house.

4. _____ You have probably never been a customer.

B. Check (✔) the examples of **customers**.

☐ people who shop at a clothing store

☐ people who go to the beach

☐ people who eat at a restaurant

☐ people who go to a beauty salon

☐ people who attend a church

Challenge Words

Check (✔) the words you already know.

☐ agent   ☐ client   ☐ seller   ☐ vendor

☐ broker   ☐ merchant   ☐ shopper

396. People Who Work in Offices

Check (✔) the word if you already know it. Then, listen and repeat.

Track 1

☐ secretary

TR 1

Definition

A **secretary** is a person whose job is to type letters, answer the telephone, and do other office work.

Check Your Understanding

A. Check (✔) the things that a **secretary** might do.

☐ answer the telephone

☐ greet visitors to an office

☐ mop the floor of the office

☐ make photocopies

☐ fix the electricity in the office

B. Choose the sentence that uses the underlined word correctly.

1. a. The <u>secretary</u> in our office is in charge of hiring and firing the employees.

   b. The <u>secretary</u> makes copies for everybody in our office.

2. a. The <u>secretary</u> answers the telephone for the manager.

   b. The <u>secretary</u> cooks lunch for the employees.

3. a. <u>Secretaries</u> must know how to fly airplanes.

   b. <u>Secretaries</u> work in offices.

Challenge Words

Check (✔) the words you already know.

☐ clerk   ☐ receptionist   ☐ typist

397. Occupations Associated with Transportation

Check (✔) the word if you already know it. Then, listen and repeat.

Track 1

TR 1

Definition

A **pilot** is a person who flies an aircraft, such as an airplane or a jet plane.

☐ **pilot**

Check Your Understanding

A. Check (✔) the things that a **pilot** might control.

☐ a car   ☐ an elevator

☐ an airplane   ☐ a helicopter

☐ a jet   ☐ a train

B. Write **T** for **true statements** and **F** for **false statements**.

1. _____ To be a pilot, you need to be able to see very well.

2. _____ If you know how to drive a car, you can be a pilot.

3. _____ A pilot might control an airliner or a fighter jet.

Challenge Words

Check (✔) the words you already know.

☐ aviator   ☐ driver   ☐ porter   ☐ skipper

186. Attractiveness

Check (✔) the words you already know. Then, listen and repeat.

Tracks 1–6

☐ **lovely**

TR 1

☐ **beautiful**

TR 2

☐ **pretty**

TR 3

Check Your Understanding

A. Underline the correct word to complete each sentence.

1. Gina told me that I have very (**pretty / ugly**) smile. She wanted to know why I was in such a good mood.

2. How (**cute / handsome**) your young daughter is! I love her curly hair.

3. Do you think that Michael is (**handsome / beautiful**)? Isabel wants to go on a date with him.

4. Jennifer looked (**lovely / handsome**) on her wedding day.

5. I dressed up like an (**ugly / handsome**) witch for the Halloween party.

6. Alex told his mother that she is (**ugly / beautiful**), and it made her smile.

○ **ugly**

TR 4

○ **handsome**

TR 5

Definitions

A **beautiful** person is very attractive to look at.

A **cute** person is pretty. **Cute** is often used to describe children.

A **handsome** man has an attractive face.

When someone is **lovely**, that person is beautiful, very nice, or very enjoyable.

A **pretty** person looks nice and is attractive in a delicate way.

When someone is **ugly**, that person is very unpleasant to look at.

○ **cute**

TR 6

B. Write **T** for **true statements** and **F** for **false statements**.

1. _____ When a person is beautiful, that person is thought to be very pretty.

2. _____ You can use the word pretty to describe a person who is unpleasant to look at.

3. _____ The word ugly means the same as beautiful.

4. _____ When someone is lovely, that person is not beautiful.

5. _____ A cute baby is very ugly.

6. _____ Male movie stars are often described as handsome.

Challenge Words

Check (✔) the words you already know.

○ adorable   ○ classic   ○ exquisite   ○ gorgeous   ○ sightly

○ breathtaking   ○ elegant   ○ formal   ○ hideous   ○ unattractive

187. Physical Trait (Size)

Check (✔) the words you already know. Then, listen and repeat.

Tracks 1–6

⬜ **chubby**

TR 1

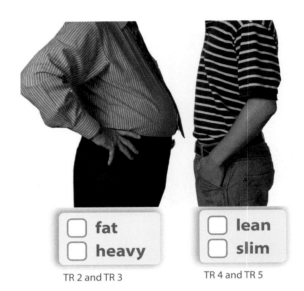

⬜ **fat**
⬜ **heavy**

TR 2 and TR 3

⬜ **lean**
⬜ **slim**

TR 4 and TR 5

Check Your Understanding

A. Choose the sentence that correctly uses the underlined word.

1. a. If you exercise and eat a healthy diet, you will not get <u>fat</u>.

   b. If you exercise and eat a healthy diet, you will get <u>fat</u>.

2. a. My older cousin is skinny and <u>heavy</u>. He plays on his school's football team.

   b. My older cousin is strong and <u>heavy</u>. He plays on his school's football team.

3. a. Our neighbor's baby has cute, <u>chubby</u> legs.

   b. Our neighbor's baby has <u>chubby</u> legs because she doesn't eat a lot.

4. a. Matt is tall and very <u>lean</u>. He is in good shape.

   b. Matt is tall and very <u>lean</u>. He is chubby.

5. a. Jack has always weighed too much. He has always been very <u>skinny</u>.

   b. Jack has never weighed too much. He has always been very <u>skinny</u>.

6. a. That dress looks nice on you. It makes you look very <u>slim</u>.

   b. That dress looks horrible on you. It makes you look very <u>slim</u>.

☐ **skinny**

TR 6

Definitions

A **chubby** person is slightly fat or plump.

A person who is **fat** is overweight or heavy.

A **heavy** person weighs a lot.

A **lean** person is thin, and usually healthy.

Someone who is **skinny** is very thin or too thin.

When you are **slim**, your body is thin in an attractive way.

B. Match each word to the correct description. One description will not be used.

1. _____ fat
2. _____ heavy
3. _____ chubby
4. _____ lean
5. _____ skinny
6. _____ slim

a. a little bit fat

b. thin in an attractive way

c. thin and healthy

d. a person who weighs a lot or is fat

e. tiny and delicate

f. a person that is overweight

g. very thin or too thin

Challenge Words

Check (✔) the words you already know.

☐ burly   ☐ husky   ☐ plump   ☐ slender   ☐ stout

☐ dainty   ☐ obese   ☐ pudgy   ☐ slight

253. Physical Characteristics

Check (✔) the words you already know. Then, listen and repeat.

Tracks 1–10

- ☐ **weakness**

TR 1

- ☐ **clumsy**

TR 2

- ☐ **beauty**

TR 3

- ☐ **might**
- ☐ **power**
- ☐ **strength**

TR 4, TR 5, and TR 6

Check Your Understanding

A. Circle the correct word to complete each sentence.

1. Sara and Joe enjoyed the _____ of the sky at sunset.
   a. strength   b. beauty   c. power

2. Tina is sometimes _____. She knocked over a glass of milk today.
   a. strong   b. weak   c. clumsy

3. Brian knows that he needs to go to the gym every day if he wants to be _____.
   a. strong   b. weak   c. clumsy

4. The old man was so _____ that he could no longer climb the stairs.
   a. strong   b. athletic   c. weak

5. Louis has the _____ to lift the heavy bricks over his head.
   a. weakness   b. power   c. clumsy

6. Paul is feeling _____ in his right hand, so he is going to the doctor.
   a. beauty   b. might   c. weakness

7. The child tried with all his _____ to pick up his older brother, but he could not.
   a. weakness   b. health   c. might

8. The doctor said that I am in very good _____ because of my good diet and exercise.
   a. strength   b. health   c. weakness

9. Eric is the most _____ person that I know. He is on both the tennis and track teams.
   a. athletic   b. strong   c. clumsy

10. Elizabeth did not have the _____ to get out of bed. She was very ill.
    a. beauty   b. strength   c. weakness

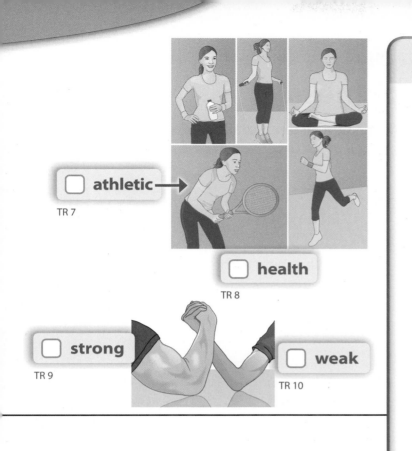

athletic
TR 7

health
TR 8

strong
TR 9

weak
TR 10

Definitions

A person who is **athletic** is good at any type of physical sport, exercise, or game.

Beauty is something that is pleasing to the senses or has the quality of being beautiful.

A **clumsy** person does not move in a very easy way and often breaks things.

Health is the condition of a person's body.

Might is power or strength.

Power is your physical strength or the ability to do something.

Your **strength** is how physically strong you are.

Someone who is **strong** is healthy with good muscles.

Someone who is **weak** is not healthy or does not have strong muscles.

Someone who feels **weakness** does not feel strength.

B. Write **T** for **true statements** and **F** for **false statements**.

1. _____ If you feel weakness in your body, you have extra strength.

2. _____ An athletic person does not like sports.

3. _____ If you do something with all your might, you put a lot of power into it.

4. _____ If someone says that you are a beauty, it means that you are good at sports.

5. _____ A person who is weak could probably lift a television set without help.

6. _____ You might lift weights to become strong.

7. _____ Someone who can lift a piano has a lot of power.

8. _____ A person who is clumsy does not break things often.

9. _____ Health is the condition of a person's body.

10. _____ You need to have strength to run a long distance.

Challenge Words

Check (✔) the words you already know.

☐ agility   ☐ frail   ☐ muscular   ☐ puny   ☐ scrawny

☐ awkward   ☐ gawky   ☐ powerful   ☐ rickety   ☐ vigor

407. Neatness / Sloppiness

Check (✔) the word if you already know it. Then, listen and repeat.

Track 1

☐ **neat**

TR 1

Definition

A **neat** person is organized and clean, and has everything in the correct place.

Check Your Understanding

A. Check (✔) each example of when it is important to look **neat**.

☐ at a job interview

☐ when going to bed

☐ while playing soccer

☐ when attending a meeting

☐ at a fancy dinner

B. Write **T** for **true statements** and **F** for **false statements**.

1. _____ If a person is neat, he never brushes his hair.

2. _____ If your room is neat, your bed is made and things are put away.

3. _____ Your mother probably wants you to keep the house neat.

4. _____ If you pick up your clothes from yesterday off the floor and wear them, you will probably look neat.

Challenge Words

Check (✔) the words you already know.

☐ prim   ☐ shipshape   ☐ sloppy   ☐ tangle   ☐ tidy

219. Alphabet and Letters

Check (✔) the words you already know. Then, listen and repeat.

Tracks 1–5

☐ **letter**
TR 1

Definitions

An **alphabet** is a set of letters used in a language.

A **consonant** is one of the letters of the alphabet that is not a vowel. For example, *b*, *c*, and *m* are consonants.

A **letter** is a written symbol that represents a sound in a language.

A **symbol** is a written character that is part of a language.

A **vowel** is one of the letters in the alphabet that is not a consonant. The letters *a*, *e*, *i*, *o*, and *u*, and sometimes *y* are **vowels**.

☐ **alphabet**
TR 2

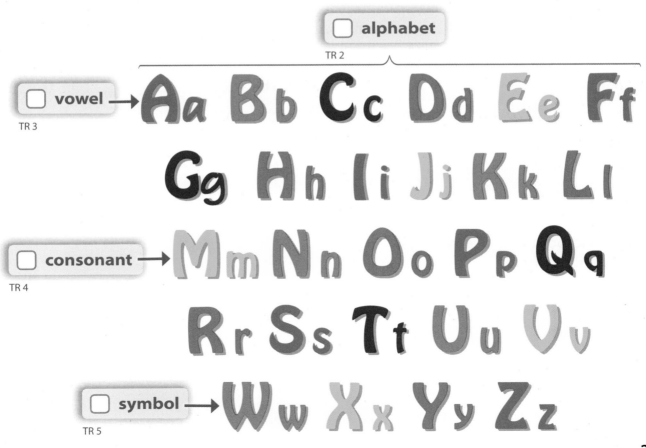

☐ **vowel** →
TR 3

☐ **consonant** →
TR 4

☐ **symbol** →
TR 5

A a B b C c D d E e F f
G g H h I i J j K k L l
M m N n O o P p Q q
R r S s T t U u V v
W w X x Y y Z z

235

Check Your Understanding

A. Choose the correct word to complete each sentence.

1. D is the fourth _____ of the alphabet.

   a. vowel   b. alphabet   c. letter

2. The letters A, E, I, O, and U are examples of _____.

   a. consonants   b. alphabets   c. vowels

3. The letter P is a consonant, but it is also an example of a _____.

   a. symbol   b. alphabet   c. vowel

4. F, K, S, and T are examples of _____.

   a. vowels   b. alphabets   c. consonants

5. The letters A through Z make up the _____.

   a. vowel   b. alphabet   c. letter

B. Complete the paragraph with the correct words from the word bank.

alphabet	letters	vowels
consonants	symbol	

   The English (1) _____ has twenty-six (2) _____.
Five letters are (3) _____, and the rest are (4) _____. When
you put them together, they form words. A letter can also be a (5) _____ that
represents a written character of a language. For example, *x* is the symbol for the twenty-fourth
letter of the alphabet.

Challenge Words

Check (✔) the words you already know.

☐ alpha   ☐ beta   ☐ code   ☐ italic

☐ alphabetically   ☐ Braille   ☐ cuneiform

238. Words, Phrases, and Sentences

Check (✔) the words you already know. Then, listen and repeat.

Tracks 1–6

He owns a green car.
↑   ↑   ↑
verb   adjective   noun

Definitions

An **adjective** is a word such as *green* that describes a person or thing. **Adjectives** usually come before nouns or after verbs like *be* or *feel*.

An **adverb** is a word such as *quickly* or *very* that adds information about an action, event, or situation. Many **adverbs** end in the letters *-ly*.

A **noun** is a word such as *car* or *road* that is used for talking about a person, a place, or a thing.

A **sentence** is a group of words that tells you something or asks a question. When a complete **sentence** is written, it begins with a capital letter and ends with a period.

A **verb** is a word such as *owns* or *drives* that is used to show an action that someone or something does.

A **word** is a unit of language with meaning.

sentence

He drives quickly down the road.
↑   ↑
adverb   word

- ☐ **verb**
  TR 1
- ☐ **adjective**
  TR 2
- ☐ **noun**
  TR 3
- ☐ **sentence**
  TR 4
- ☐ **adverb**
  TR 5
- ☐ **word**
  TR 6

Check Your Understanding

A. Circle the correct word to complete each sentence.

1. Please remember to put a period at the end of each _____ in your report.

   a. word   b. sentence   c. verb

2. Tim is my best <u>friend</u>. The underlined word in this sentence is _____ .

   a. a verb   b. an adjective   c. a noun

3. The <u>furry</u> dog watched the children play. The underlined word in this sentence is _____ .

   a. an adjective   b. a noun   c. a verb

4. Mr. Wilson <u>speaks</u> English and Spanish fluently. The underlined word in this sentence is _____ .

   a. a noun   b. an adjective   c. a verb

5. The old man <u>slowly</u> walked down the sidewalk. The underlined word in this sentence is _____ .

   a. an adverb   b. a verb   c. an adjective

6. *Green, car,* and *owns* are all examples of _____ .

   a. words   b. sentences   c. nouns

B. Write **T** for **true statements** and **F** for **false statements**.

1. _____ Words have no meaning.

2. _____ A word is made up of several sentences.

3. _____ An adjective is a word that describes a person or a thing.

4. _____ An adverb is a word that describes a person or thing.

5. _____ *Swim, eat,* and *dance* are all examples of verbs.

6. _____ A noun is a word for a person, a place, or a thing.

Challenge Words

Check (✔) the words you already know.

☐ antonym   ☐ homonym   ☐ prefix   ☐ pronoun   ☐ suffix

☐ conjunction   ☐ phrase   ☐ preposition   ☐ subject   ☐ synonym

286. Language Conventions

Check (✔) the words you already know. Then, listen and repeat.

Tracks 1–4

Definitions

A **comma** is the punctuation mark (,).
A **comma** separates a group of words in a sentence or list. It also indicates a pause in a sentence.

Language is a system of sounds and written symbols that people of a particular country or region use in talking or writing.

A **period** is the punctuation mark (.).
A **period** ends a sentence.

The **vocabulary** of a language is all the words in it or all the words you know.

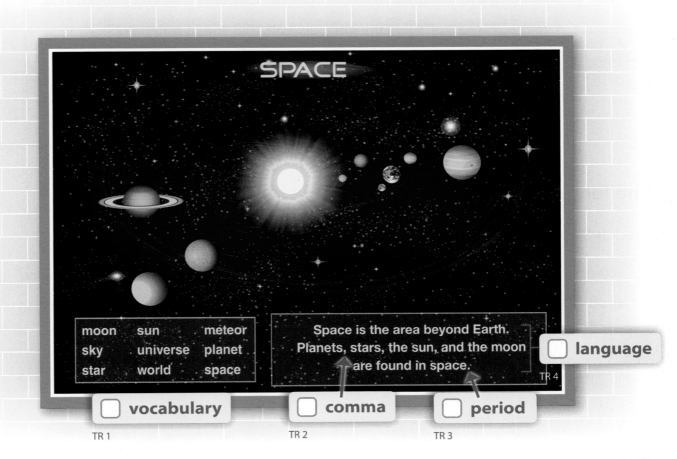

SPACE

moon	sun	meteor
sky	universe	planet
star	world	space

Space is the area beyond Earth.
Planets, stars, the sun, and the moon are found in space.

TR 4

☐ language

☐ vocabulary

TR 1

☐ comma

TR 2

☐ period

TR 3

Check Your Understanding

A. Circle the correct answer.

1. Read this sentence: **The dog was big loud friendly and fun.**

   What is missing from the sentence above?

   a. commas

   b. language

   c. periods

   d. vocabulary

2. Which sentence below gives the **best** meaning of the word *vocabulary*?

   a. letters that you need to write

   b. symbols that are used in a language

   c. words that make up a language

   d. numbers that are used in math

3. Read the following sentence: **Janet loves to watch movies**

   What is missing from the sentence above?

   a. a comma

   b. language

   c. a period

   d. vocabulary

4. What would **best** complete the following sentence?

   Ada speaks three _____ : Russian, Spanish, and English.

   a. putting a comma in the blank

   b. putting a period in the blank

   c. putting the word **vocabularies** in the blank

   d. putting the word **languages** in the blank

B. Match each word to the correct description. One description will not be used.

1. _____ comma

2. _____ language

3. _____ period

4. _____ vocabulary

a. a punctuation mark that ends a statement

b. the correct way to speak a language

c. a punctuation mark that shows a pause in a sentence

d. the words that make up a language

e. a system of sounds and letters that is used for communication

Challenge Words

Check (✔) the words you already know.

- [ ] accent
- [ ] apostrophe
- [ ] colon
- [ ] emphasis
- [ ] grammar
- [ ] parenthesis
- [ ] pronunciation
- [ ] punctuation
- [ ] slang
- [ ] tense

211. Courage and Loyalty

Check (✔) the words you already know. Then, listen and repeat.

 Tracks 1–5

☐ honest

TR 1

Definitions

Someone who is **brave** is willing to do things that are dangerous and does not show fear in dangerous situations.

Courage is a quality that someone shows when they are not afraid.

When someone is **heroic**, he or she shows great courage.

When someone is **honest**, that person tells the truth, and does not steal or cheat.

A **loyal** person is faithful to his or her friends, beliefs, or country, even in difficult times.

☐ brave

TR 2

☐ courage

TR 3

☐ heroic

TR 4

They are **loyal** fans of their favorite soccer team.

☐ loyal

TR 5

Check Your Understanding

A. Choose the correct word from the word bank to complete each sentence.

| brave | courage | heroic | honest | loyal |

1. Alan showed great courage during the _____ rescue of the girl from the rough waters.

2. Jack was not afraid to go climbing on the cliffs. He is a very _____ person.

3. Patty has been a _____ customer at that store for almost eight years.

4. Please be _____ with me, and do not lie.

5. The little girl must have a lot of _____ to get up in front of this crowd to sing.

B. Circle the correct word to complete each sentence.

1. Is Andy _____ enough to spend a whole week camping alone?

   a. loyal   b. brave   c. honest

2. Whenever you see Lola, you will see her _____ sister right behind her.

   a. honest   b. courage   c. loyal

3. Sara is always _____, so everyone trusts her.

   a. honest   b. heroic   c. loyal

4. It was very _____ when Rob rescued the cat from the tree.

   a. loyal   b. courage   c. heroic

5. It takes a lot of _____ to stand up to a bully, but you will be glad you did.

   a. courage   b. loyal   c. heroic

Challenge Words

Check (✔) the words you already know.

| ☐ adventurous | ☐ bold | ☐ chivalry | ☐ devotion | ☐ obedience |
| ☐ allegiance | ☐ bravery | ☐ courageous | ☐ gallant | ☐ valor |

228. Goodness and Kindness

Check (✔) the words you already know. Then, listen and repeat.

 Tracks 1–9

☐ **respectful**

TR 1

☐ **nice**

TR 2

☐ **kind**

TR 3

☐ **grateful**
☐ **thankful**

TR 4 and TR 5

Definitions

Someone who is **considerate** thinks about and cares about the feelings of other people.

Someone who is **courteous** is polite.

Someone who is **gentle** is kind, mild, and calm.

When you are **grateful** for something that someone gives you or does for you, you feel glad and you want to thank them.

Someone who is **kind** is friendly and helpful.

When someone is **nice**, they are friendly and pleasant.

A **polite** person behaves with respect toward other people.

When you are **respectful**, you are polite to people.

When you are **thankful**, you are very grateful and glad that something has happened.

☐ **considerate**

TR 6

☐ **gentle**

TR 7

☐ **courteous**
☐ **polite**

TR 8 and TR 9

Check Your Understanding

A. Write T for true statements and F for false statements.

1. _____ You would be thankful to the person who rescued your cat from a tree.

2. _____ It is considerate to make a lot of noise late at night.

3. _____ If somebody pushes you, that person is being gentle.

4. _____ If you help a friend study for a test, he will probably be grateful to you.

5. _____ A person who is kind is very nice.

6. _____ A nice person is never courteous.

7. _____ It is polite to talk loudly in a movie theater.

8. _____ A respectful student follows the rules.

9. _____ It is courteous to interrupt others while they are talking.

B. Underline the correct word to complete each sentence.

1. It was so (**nice / thankful**) of you to make us dinner.

2. Peter has been very (**kind / gentle**) to me. He helped me move and found me a job.

3. I am (**respectful / thankful**) that it did not rain today so that we could go to the baseball game.

4. It is (**grateful / polite**) to wait your turn in a line.

5. In many cultures, it is considered (**respectful / gentle**) to take off your hat at the dinner table.

6. Thomas was (**grateful / courteous**) that his uncle gave him a summer job.

7. It was not very (**considerate / thankful**) to take the last slice of pizza without asking if anyone else wanted it.

8. Please be (**gentle / considerate**) with the baby.

9. The (**thankful / courteous**) boy held the door open for others as they walked in.

Challenge Words

Check (✔) the words you already know.

- ☐ affectionate
- ☐ generous
- ☐ kindness
- ☐ sympathetic
- ☐ thoughtful
- ☐ amiable
- ☐ hospitality
- ☐ sensitive
- ☐ tender
- ☐ unselfish

278. Pride and Confidence

Check (✔) the words you already know. Then, listen and repeat.

Tracks 1–5

JOB FAIR

☐ **confident**

TR 1

☐ **proud**

TR 2

Definitions

When you are **certain** about something, you strongly believe that it is true and have no doubts about it.

When you are **confident** about something, you are certain that the result will be good.

When you are **hopeful**, you think that something that you want will probably happen.

When you feel **proud**, you feel pleased and satisfied about an accomplishment.

When you are **sure** that something is true, you are certain about it.

There is a 100% chance of rain today.

☐ **hopeful**

TR 3

☐ **certain**
☐ **sure**

TR 4 and TR 5

Check Your Understanding

A. Underline the correct word to complete each sentence.

1. I am (**proud / sure**) that the party starts at 6 o'clock. It says the time on the invitation.

2. Eva is (**certain / hopeful**) that she will not attend the concert this Friday because she has to babysit her little brother.

3. Tina is (**confident / proud**) that the interview went well, and she thinks she will get the job.

4. Lynn felt very (**proud / sure**) of her son when he got into college.

5. All the actresses were (**hopeful / proud**) that they would get called back for another audition.

B. Write **T** for **true statements** and **F** for **false statements**.

1. _____ You have just finished a difficult test. You are sure that you got an A.

2. _____ If doctors are hopeful about a patient's progress, they fear that the patient will get worse.

3. _____ If you see your friend at work, you can be certain that she is there.

4. _____ Your parents are probably proud of you when you get in trouble at school.

5. _____ If you are confident that you are good at a task, you think you do a great job on it.

Challenge Words

Check (✔) the words you already know.

- ☐ conceit
- ☐ confidence
- ☐ frank
- ☐ haughty
- ☐ pride
- ☐ smug
- ☐ vain

294. Dependability and Eagerness

Check (✔) the words you already know. Then, listen and repeat.

Tracks 1–4

Definitions

Someone who is **active** moves around a lot.

When you are **busy**, you are working hard, so that you are not free to do anything else.

When you are **eager** to do something, you want to do it very much.

Responsible people can be trusted to do something and behave in a proper and sensible way.

☐ **busy**

TR 1

☐ **eager**

TR 2

☐ **active**

TR 3

☐ **responsible**

TR 4

247

Check Your Understanding

A. Match each word to the best example. One example will not be used.

1. _____ active
2. _____ busy
3. _____ eager
4. _____ responsible

a. Jill has never been late to work. Her boss knows that she will always be on time.

b. Nancy really wants to work and will take any job she finds.

c. Grandma goes to a swimming class three mornings each week.

d. Michael has two jobs and goes to school, so he cannot meet us for dinner.

e. Whatever Jaime says is always true.

B. Circle the correct word to complete each sentence.

1. Paul is _____ to meet new people, so he goes to many social events.

    a. responsible   b. busy   c. eager

2. Amy is very _____ . She runs track, swims, and plays softball.

    a. eager   b. active   c. responsible

3. Do you think that Tracy is _____ enough to babysit for our twin daughters?

    a. busy   b. active   c. responsible

4. Between school and work, Anne is too _____ to spend any time with her friends.

    a. busy   b. responsible   c. eager

Challenge Words

Check (✔) the words you already know.

☐ ambitious   ☐ diligent   ☐ productive   ☐ responsibility   ☐ trustworthy

☐ credible   ☐ enthusiasm   ☐ reliable   ☐ thorough   ☐ zest

295. Instability

Check (✔) the words you already know. Then, listen and repeat.

Tracks 1–3

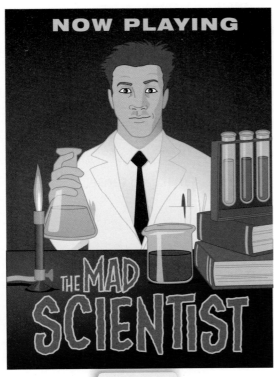

☐ **mad**

TR 1

Definitions

Someone who is **crazy** is very strange or does something that is foolish and makes little sense.

Mad behavior is wild and uncontrolled.

Wild behavior is uncontrolled or excited.

☐ **wild**

TR 3

He must be **crazy** to talk on his cell phone while driving. It's very dangerous.

☐ **crazy**

TR 2

Check Your Understanding

A. Match each word to the correct description. One description will not be used.

1. _____ crazy
2. _____ mad
3. _____ wild

a. excited behavior

b. acting in a foolish way

c. acting in a way that is rushed

d. wild and uncontrollable behavior

B. Underline the correct word to complete each sentence.

1. Some people like to swim in the ocean with sharks, but I think that is (**crazy** / **wild**).

2. The crowd went (**mad** / **wild**) when the football players ran onto the field.

3. In this story, the land is ruled by a (**wild** / **mad**) king, whose ideas make no sense.

Challenge Words

Check (✔) the words you already know.

☐ amuck   ☐ fickle   ☐ giddy   ☐ uncontrolled

☐ fanatic   ☐ frantic   ☐ hectic   ☐ unstable

332. Independence and Freedom

Check (✔) the words you already know. Then, listen and repeat.

Tracks 1–3

☐ **free**

TR 1

Definitions

Someone who is **free** is not controlled by rules or other people.

Liberty is state of being able to live and act freely and in the way that you want to.

A person that is **obedient** does what they are told to do.

☐ **liberty**

TR 2

☐ **obedient**

TR 3

251

Check Your Understanding

A. Choose the sentence that correctly uses the underlined word.

1. a. Robby is <u>free</u> to go out with his friends whenever he wants to.

   b. Robby is <u>free</u> and must stay in his room.

2. a. People have the <u>liberty</u> to be punished when they break the law.

   b. People in this country have the <u>liberty</u> to choose the job they want.

3. a. The doctor said to take two pills a day, and Jon did. He was <u>obedient</u>.

   b. The doctor said to take two pills a day, and Jon took one. He was <u>obedient</u>.

B. Choose the correct word from the word bank to complete each sentence.

free	liberty	obedient

1. Maria's dog is very _____ , and can sit, lie down, and roll over when she asks him to.

2. In this country, everyone has the _____ to practice the religion of his or her choice.

3. You are _____ to say what you think during today's debate.

Challenge Words

Check (✔) the words you already know.

☐ dependent   ☐ independent   ☐ voluntary

55 NONPHYSICAL TRAITS OF PEOPLE

350. Shyness

Check (✔) the words you already know. Then, listen and repeat.

Tracks 1–2

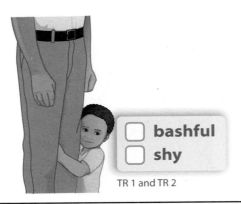

- ☐ bashful
- ☐ shy

TR 1 and TR 2

Definitions

Someone who is **bashful** is shy and is afraid to talk to people.

If you are **shy**, you are nervous and do not like to talk to people that you do not know well.

Check Your Understanding

A. Write **T** for **true statements** and **F** for **false statements**.

1. _____ Someone who is bashful is very friendly with new people.

2. _____ Someone who is shy gets nervous in front of a new group.

3. _____ A child might be bashful around a person that they are not familiar with.

4. _____ A shy person is probably happy to speak to large groups.

B. Circle the correct answer.

1. When might a person be bashful?

   a. on the first day of school   b. at home with his mother   c. playing with his toys

2. Which activity would a shy person <u>not</u> like to do?

   a. read a book in her room   b. have lunch with her sister   c. go to a big party

3. If a person is bashful, she might do which of these?

   a. give a speech   b. avoid crowds   c. go on a group hike

4. If a person is shy, he might do which of these?

   a. hide from strangers   b. take part in a play   c. make new friends easily

Challenge Words

Check (✔) the words you already know.

☐ helpless   ☐ meek   ☐ mild   ☐ skittish   ☐ timid

351. Dishonesty

Check (✔) the words you already know. Then, listen and repeat.

Tracks 1–3

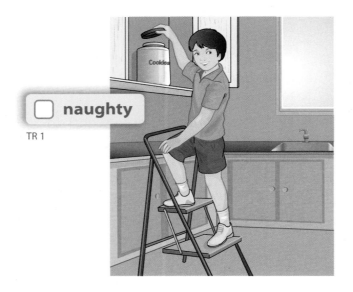

☐ **naughty**

TR 1

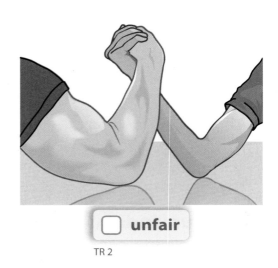

☐ **unfair**

TR 2

Check Your Understanding

A. Write **T** for **true statements** and **F** for **false statements**.

1. _____ An unfair person treats everyone equally.

2. _____ A naughty child disobeys the rules.

3. _____ A dishonest person always tells the truth.

4. _____ A naughty child always behaves nicely.

My dog ate my homework.

☐ **dishonest**

TR 3

Definitions

A **dishonest** person is a person who does not tell the truth.

A **naughty** child behaves badly or does not do what someone tells him to do.

An **unfair** person does not treat people in an equal way or in the right way. An **unfair** situation happens when people are not treated in the same way.

B. Complete the sentences.

1. A naughty child _____.

2. A dishonest person _____.

3. An unfair situation _____.

Challenge Words

Check (✔) the words you already know.

☐ cunning   ☐ mischief   ☐ mischievous   ☐ sly   ☐ traitor

385. Lack of Initiative

Check (✔) the word if you already know it. Then, listen and repeat.

Track 1

☐ **lazy**

TR 1

Definition

When someone is **lazy**, that person does not want to work.

Check Your Understanding

A. Check (✔) the sentences that describe a **lazy** person.

☐ A person who works two jobs and goes to school

☐ A person who spends the weekends lying on the couch

☐ A person who does not have a job but is looking hard to find one

☐ A person who needs money but does not want to work

☐ A person who does no schoolwork

B. Circle the correct answer.

1. When is it okay to be a lazy person?

   a. when you have to study   b. when you are tired   c. when you are at work

2. What problems might a lazy person have?

   a. no achievements   b. no time to do work   c. *a* and *b*

3. What do lazy people like to do?

   a. They like to clean.   b. They like to be very busy.   c. They like to do no work.

Challenge Words

Check (✔) the words you already know.

☐ casual   ☐ dormant   ☐ idle   ☐ lax   ☐ listless

386. Luck and Success

Check (✔) the word if you already know it. Then, listen and repeat.

Track 1

□ **lucky**

TR 1

Definition

You say that someone is **lucky** when they have good luck or good fortune.

Check Your Understanding

A. Check (✔) the sentences that describe a **lucky** person.

□ A person loses his phone and breaks his arm in the same week.

□ A person suddenly is offered a new and better job.

□ A person finds $200.00 on the sidewalk.

□ A person wins a prize at a raffle.

□ A person's dog runs away.

B. Write **T** for **true statements** and **F** for **false statements**.

1. _____ You are lucky when you do poorly on a test that you studied for.

2. _____ You are lucky when you get an A on a test that you did not study for.

3. _____ You are lucky if you lose a diamond ring.

4. _____ You are lucky if you are not hurt after a very bad car accident.

Challenge Words

Check (✔) the words you already know.

□ successful   □ unfortunate

387. Stubbornness and Strictness

Check (✔) the word if you already know it. Then, listen and repeat.

Track 1

Shh! No talking in the library.

☐ **strict**

TR 1

Definition

A **strict** person expects rules to be obeyed.

Check Your Understanding

A. Circle the correct answer.

1. Which is an example of a strict classroom rule?

   a. If you are late to class three times, you have to stay after school.

   b. If you are late to class one time, you have to stay after school.

2. Which of the following is an example of a strict rule?

   a. You can go to the movies with friends after you finish your homework.

   b. You must be home at 10:00. If you are one minute late, you cannot go to the party tomorrow.

3. Which is an example of a strict school dress code?

   a. You can wear anything you want to.

   b. You can wear only black pants and a white shirt.

B. Write **T** for **true statements** and **F** for **false statements**.

1. _____ A strict person does not like rules.

2. _____ If you never follow the rules, people will say that you are strict.

3. _____ A strict person expects the rules to be followed.

Challenge Words

Check (✔) the words you already know.

☐ grave   ☐ severe   ☐ stern   ☐ stubborn

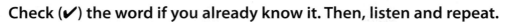

388. Spirituality

Check (✔) the word if you already know it. Then, listen and repeat.

Track 1

Many people consider Mother Theresa to be a **holy** person.

☐ **holy**

TR 1

> ### Definition
> A **holy** person is religious and morally good.

Check Your Understanding

A. Circle the correct answer.

1. Which activity is a holy person <u>not</u> likely to do?

   a. speak badly of another person   c. pray for a friend

   b. help others   d. go to church

2. Which of the following things is <u>not</u> holy?

   a. a bird   c. a priest

   b. a nun   d. a minister

3. Which of the following is **holy** to some people?

   a. a cape   c. a clock

   b. a church   d. a carpet

B. Circle five words from the box that are most associated with the word **holy**.

God	lunch	pray	sit	nun
church	notebook	laugh	work	religion

Challenge Words

Check (✔) the words you already know.

☐ divine   ☐ religious   ☐ skeptic   ☐ supernatural

☐ pious   ☐ sacred   ☐ spiritual

259

389. Caution

Check (✔) the word if you already know it. Then, listen and repeat.

Track 1

☐ careful

Definition

When you are **careful**, you are aware of danger and do things to make sure you remain safe.

Check Your Understanding

A. Check (✔) the examples of someone being **careful**.

☐ putting on a helmet and knee pads before riding a bicycle

☐ throwing your clothes on the floor

☐ checking that you turned the stove off before you leave the house

☐ making a cake without a recipe

☐ looking both ways before you cross the street

B. Write **T** for **true statements** and **F** for **false statements**.

1. _____ Your parents want you to be careful when you are cooking in the kitchen.

2. _____ If you do not wear your seatbelt in the car, you are being careful.

3. _____ You should be careful not to step on the piece of broken glass.

Challenge Words

Check (✔) the words you already know.

☐ careless   ☐ lax   ☐ prudent   ☐ slack   ☐ suspicious

☐ gingerly   ☐ painstaking   ☐ reckless   ☐ stingy   ☐ wary

230. Disease

Check (✔) the words you already know. Then, listen and repeat.

☐ **disease**

TR 1

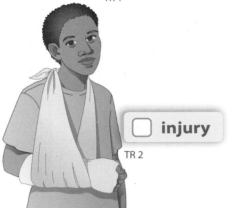

☐ **injury**

TR 2

Definitions

A **disease** is an illness that affects people, animals, or plants.

A person's **health** is the condition of that person's body and mind.

Someone who is **ill** is not in good health.

An **injury** is damage to a person's or an animal's body.

When you are **sick**, you are not well.

When you are **well**, you have good health.

☐ **health**

TR 3

☐ **well**

TR 4

☐ **ill**
☐ **sick**

TR 5 and TR 6

Check Your Understanding

A. Underline the correct word to complete each sentence.

1. Some (**diseases** / **health**) can be treated with medicines, and even cured.

2. Rachel has been out of school for over a week because she is (**sick** / **well**).

3. Charlie's (**injury** / **disease**) happened when he got hit hard during a football game.

4. The nurse goes from room to room, helping the (**ill** / **well**) people feel better.

5. Smoking can damage a person's (**disease** / **health**).

6. I promise that if you take this medicine, you will feel (**ill** / **well**) in no time.

B. Write **T** for **true statements** and **F** for **false statements**.

1. _____ You might want to send a "get well" message to a friend who is sick.

2. _____ A person who is ill is in good health.

3. _____ A disease is an illness that affects plants and animals.

4. _____ A person with an injury is in good health.

5. _____ If you want to know how your health is, you should talk to your teacher.

6. _____ When you are sick, you should stay in bed and get plenty of rest.

Challenge Words

Check (✔) the words you already know.

☐ ailment ☐ contagious ☐ famine ☐ plague ☐ symptom
☐ condition ☐ epidemic ☐ infection ☐ sickness ☐ wholesome

231. Medicine

Check (✔) the words you already know. Then, listen and repeat.

Tracks 1–6

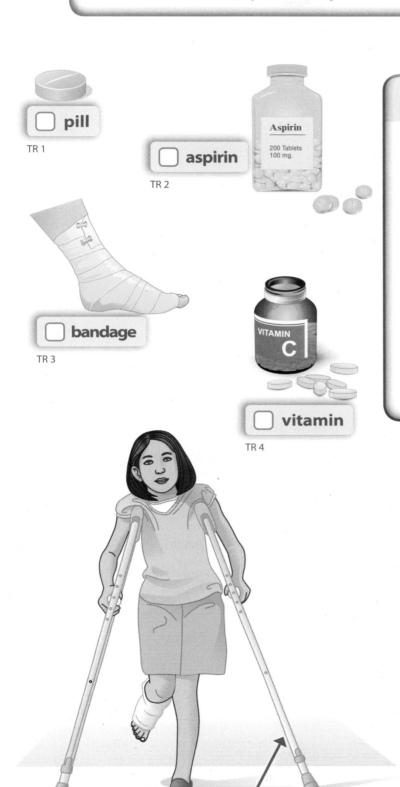

☐ **pill**
TR 1

☐ **aspirin**
TR 2

☐ **bandage**
TR 3

☐ **vitamin**
TR 4

☐ **crutch**
TR 5

Definitions

Aspirin is a mild drug that reduces pain and fever.

A **bandage** is a long strip of cloth that is wrapped around an injured part of your body to protect or support it.

A **crutch** is a long stick used for support when you are injured.

Medicine is a substance used to treat or cure an illness.

A **pill** is a small, solid, round piece of medicine that you swallow.

Vitamins are substances in foods or in pills that you need in order to stay healthy.

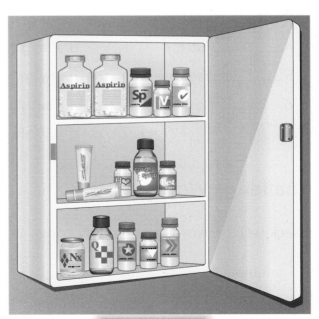

☐ **medicine**
TR 6

Check Your Understanding

A. Circle the item that will be most useful in each situation.

1. Frank twisted his ankle playing basketball.

   a. bandage   b. vitamin

2. Peter has a headache.

   a. crutch   b. aspirin

3. Anna broke her leg and cannot walk.

   a. pills   b. crutches

4. Mary has a mild case of diabetes and needs medicine.

   a. pills   b. vitamins

5. Edwin is feeling very weak due to his poor diet.

   a. vitamins   b. bandages

6. The woman suffers from several different diseases.

   a. crutches   b. medicine

B. Match each word with the correct description. One description will not be used.

1. _____ pill

2. _____ aspirin

3. _____ bandage

4. _____ crutch

5. _____ medicine

6. _____ vitamin

a. a long stick that you use to support your body if your leg is injured

b. a small, round piece of medicine that you swallow

c. a shot in the arm that will prevent a future disease

d. a long piece of cloth that you use to support or cover an injury

e. any cream, pill, or syrup that you take to help you feel better

f. a substance found in foods that helps keep your body healthy

g. a small, white pill that you take if you have a fever or pain

Challenge Words

Check (✔) the words you already know.

☐ antibiotics   ☐ dose   ☐ operate   ☐ surgery   ☐ treatment

☐ diagnose   ☐ drug   ☐ remedy   ☐ therapy   ☐ vaccine

287. Symptoms

Check (✔) the words you already know. Then, listen and repeat.

 Tracks 1–4

☐ **dizzy**

TR 1

Definitions

When you feel **dizzy**, you feel that you are going to fall.

If you have a **fever** when you are sick, your body is very hot.

When you have an **itch**, you have an unpleasant feeling on your skin that makes you want to scratch it.

Pain is the feeling that you have in a part of your body because of illness or an injury.

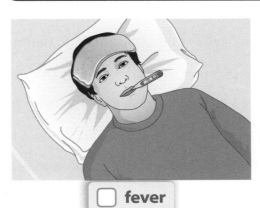

☐ **fever**

TR 2

☐ **itch**

TR 3

☐ **pain**

TR 4

Check Your Understanding

A. Choose the correct word from the word bank to complete each sentence.

dizzy	fever	itch	pain

1. Claire is going to stay home from school today because she has a _____ of 103°.
2. The _____ on my back is annoying because I cannot scratch it.
3. The small children ran in circles until they got _____.
4. Julie has been feeling _____ in her right arm, so she will not play tennis with us.

B. Choose the sentence that correctly uses the underlined word.

1. a. Sitting on the couch makes me so <u>dizzy</u> that I need to get up.

   b. Running around in circles makes me so <u>dizzy</u> that I need to sit down.

2. a. If you have a <u>fever</u>, you should take some medicine.

   b. If you have a <u>fever</u>, you should go to the party.

3. a. Steve said that the rain gave him an <u>itch</u> on his leg.

   b. Steve said that the rash gave him an <u>itch</u> on his leg.

4. a. Putting your hat on your head causes a lot of <u>pain</u>.

   b. Hitting your head on the ceiling causes a lot of <u>pain</u>.

Challenge Words

Check (✔) the words you already know.

☐ ache   ☐ impair   ☐ numb   ☐ toothache

☐ headache   ☐ nausea   ☐ sore   ☐ vomit

305. Actions Associated with Disease / Injury

Check (✔) the words you already know. Then, listen and repeat.

 Tracks 1–4

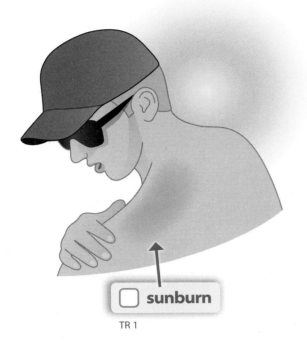

☐ **sunburn**

TR 1

Definitions

A **blister** is a raised area of skin filled with a clear liquid.

A **burn** is an injury caused by fire or something very hot.

A **scab** is a hard, dry cover that forms over the surface of a wound on your skin.

A **sunburn** is a type of burn that happens when you have spent too much time in the sun.

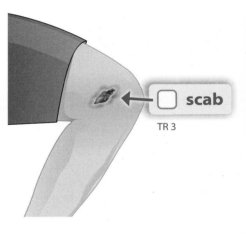

☐ **scab**

TR 3

☐ **burn**

TR 2

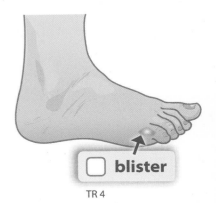

☐ **blister**

TR 4

267

Check Your Understanding

A. Circle the correct answer.

1. What is a blister filled with?
   a. a clear liquid   b. water   c. blood

2. When might you get a sunburn?
   a. after a day at the mall   b. after a day at the beach   c. after a hard day at school

3. When does a scab form on your skin?
   a. before an injury   b. after you bathe yourself   c. after an injury

4. When could you get a burn?
   a. if you touch ice   b. if you touch a hot stove   c. if you touch warm water

B. Match each word to the correct description. One description will not be used.

1. _____ blister
2. _____ burn
3. _____ scab
4. _____ sunburn

  a. an injury on your skin that comes from touching something hot

  b. the poison from a snake bite

  c. a bubble of liquid under your skin

  d. having red skin from being outside on a sunny day

  e. a hard, rough area of your skin that forms on a cut

Challenge Words

Check (✔) the words you already know.

- ☐ concussion
- ☐ infect
- ☐ poison
- ☐ venom
- ☐ wound
- ☐ gash
- ☐ paralyze
- ☐ sprain
- ☐ whiplash

371. Disabilities and Diseases

Check (✔) the words you already know. Then, listen and repeat.

Tracks 1–3

☐ **blind**

TR 1

Definitions

A **blind** person is unable to see because of injured or diseased eyes.

When you have a **cold**, you have an illness that makes liquid flow from your nose and makes you cough.

A **deaf** person is unable to hear. A **deaf** person often uses his or her hands to communicate in a special language called sign language.

☐ **deaf**

TR 3

☐ **cold**

TR 2

Check Your Understanding

A. Match each word to the best example of it. One example will not be used.

1. _____ blind
2. _____ cold
3. _____ deaf

    a. John has been coughing all night and feels terrible.

    b. George owns a trained dog that helps him find his way.

    c. Lisa is teaching her cousins sign language so that she can talk with them.

    d. Marie was born without the ability to speak.

B. Circle the correct word to complete each sentence.

1. The _____ students communicate by using sign language.

    a. blind   b. cold   c. deaf

2. Whenever I have a _____ , I stay in bed and drink lots of liquids.

    a. blind   b. cold   c. deaf

3. Some dogs are specially trained as guides to help _____ people.

    a. blind   b. cold   c. deaf

Challenge Words

Check (✔) the words you already know.

☐ blindness   ☐ influenza   ☐ mute   ☐ stress

☐ cancer   ☐ lame   ☐ starvation

404. Germs and Genes

Check (✔) the word if you already know it. Then, listen and repeat.

Track 1

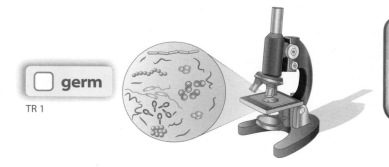

☐ **germ**

TR 1

Definition

A **germ** is a very small living thing that can cause disease or illness.

Check Your Understanding

A. Choose the sentence that correctly uses the underlined word.

1. a. Cover your mouth when you cough so you don't spread any <u>germs</u>.

   b. The table was very clean and full of <u>germs</u>.

2. a. Bert visited the sick <u>germ</u> at the hospital.

   b. You should wash your hands to remove any <u>germs</u> before you eat.

B. Write **T** for **true statements** and **F** for **false statements**.

1. _____ Germs are very large and are not alive.

2. _____ When germs get in your body, they may make you sick.

3. _____ If you brush your teeth, you can help keep germs out of your mouth.

4. _____ When you wash your hands, you are getting germs on them.

Challenge Words

Check (✔) the words you already know.

☐ bacteria   ☐ microbe   ☐ organism   ☐ virus

261. Likelihood and Certainty

Check (✔) the words you already know. Then, listen and repeat.

Tracks 1–7

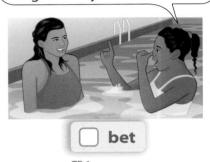

I **bet** you I can hold my breath longer than you can!

☐ **bet**

TR 1

It might be sunny this afternoon.

☐ **possible**

TR 2

I am **certain** it will rain tonight.

☐ **certain**

TR 3

☐ **miracle**

TR 4

Check Your Understanding

A. Choose the sentence that correctly uses the underlined word.

1. a. Ned <u>bet</u> his sister that he could run faster than her.

   b. Our teacher handed out <u>bets</u> to everyone in the class.

2. a. We may not go for ice cream after dinner. I am <u>certain</u> of it.

   b. We will go for ice cream after dinner. I am <u>certain</u> of it.

3. a. The talented girl had a <u>chance</u> of winning the competition.

   b. The talented girl had a competition without a <u>chance</u>.

4. a. It is <u>likely</u> that it will snow if it is hot out.

   b. It is <u>likely</u> that we will go to the beach if it is hot out.

5. a. People say that seeing a black cat brings bad <u>luck</u>.

   b. People say that seeing bad <u>luck</u> brings a black cat.

6. a. It would be a <u>miracle</u> for your garden to grow with no rain.

   b. It would be a <u>miracle</u> for a flower to grow in a garden.

7. a. If <u>possible</u>, I am a student.

   b. It is <u>possible</u> for me to speak English.

☐ **luck**

TR 5

☐ **chance**

TR 6

☐ **likely**

TR 7

Definitions

You use expressions such as "I **bet**," "I'll **bet**," and "you can **bet**" to indicate that you believe something is true.

If you are **certain** about something, you strongly believe that it is true.

If there is a **chance** that something will happen, it is possible that it will happen.

If someone or something is **likely** to do a particular thing, they will probably do it.

Luck is good things that happen to you, that have not been caused by yourself or other people.

A **miracle** is a surprising and lucky event that you cannot explain.

If it is **possible** to do something, it can be done. If it is **possible** that something is true, it might be true, although you do not know for sure.

B. Circle the correct word to complete each sentence.

1. Are you _____ that it is going to rain today? The sky is perfectly clear.
   a. certain   b. possible   c. likely

2. Jim does not have a _____ to win this game. The other golfer is the world champion.
   a. luck   b. chance   c. bet

3. I want Italian food, so it is _____ that we will go to an Italian restaurant.
   a. miracle   b. likely   c. certain

4. Rich _____ that his classmates could not finish all their work before noon.
   a. luck   b. miracle   c. bet

5. It was good _____ that Paula found a twenty-dollar bill on the street.
   a. bet   b. chance   c. luck

6. Is it _____ for you to speak more quietly?
   a. possible   b. bet   c. certain

7. This class is difficult. It would be a _____ if I got an A.
   a. certain   b. miracle   c. bet

Challenge Words

Check (✔) the words you already know.

☐ absolute   ☐ definite   ☐ fluke   ☐ mysterious   ☐ random

☐ accidental   ☐ destiny   ☐ hazard   ☐ opportunity   ☐ uncertain

289. Familiarity and Popularity

Check (✔) the words you already know. Then, listen and repeat.

Tracks 1–7

It is **common** to see pigeons at the park.

She looks **familiar** to me.

☐ **popular**

TR 1

☐ **common**

TR 2

☐ **familiar**

TR 3

Check Your Understanding

A. Write **T** for **true statements** and **F** for **false statements**.

1. _____ If you have a common name, many other people have the same name.

2. _____ When someone looks familiar, you think you have seen him before.

3. _____ It is normal for you to dress like a clown when you go to English class.

4. _____ On an ordinary night, you see fireworks in the sky.

5. _____ If someone is popular, not many people like him or her.

6. _____ If you wear your regular clothes, you put on what you wear on most days.

7. _____ On a usual morning, you might wake up, eat breakfast, and get dressed.

☐ **normal**
☐ **ordinary**

TR 4 and TR 5

Monday Tuesday Wednesday

☐ **regular**
☐ **usual**

TR 6 and TR 7

Definitions

When something is **common**, it is found in large numbers or happens often.

When someone or something is **familiar**, you have seen or heard that person or thing before.

Something that is **normal** is usual and ordinary.

Ordinary people or things are normal or common and are not special or different in a clear way.

Something or someone that is **popular** is liked by a lot of people.

Regular means normal or ordinary. A **regular** event happens often.

Usual describes what happens most often.

B. Underline the correct word to complete each sentence.

1. That girl looks so (**familiar** / **normal**) to me. I think I took an art class with her.

2. Every day, Larry orders the same thing. His (**usual** / **popular**) lunch is a hamburger and a salad.

3. Four students are named Eva in this year's class. It is a very (**common** / **usual**) name these days.

4. The students were all in their (**ordinary** / **popular**) clothes. No one was dressed up.

5. Sandra is a (**regular** / **ordinary**) customer at this coffee shop and comes in every day.

6. It is not (**normal** / **familiar**) to be so tired all of the time. Maybe you should see a doctor.

7. Lily is the most (**usual** / **popular**) girl in our class. Everyone likes her.

Challenge Words

Check (✔) the words you already know.

☐ customary   ☐ fame   ☐ obvious   ☐ recognition   ☐ typical

☐ evident   ☐ hip   ☐ prominent   ☐ standard   ☐ universal

328. Lack of Popularity / Familiarity

Check (✔) the words you already know. Then, listen and repeat.

 Tracks 1–2

☐ **private**

TR 1

☐ **secret**

TR 2

Definitions

When something is **private**, it is only for one particular person or group, and not for everyone.

When something is **secret**, only a small number of people know about it, and they do not tell anyone else.

Check Your Understanding

A. Choose the correct word from the word bank to complete each sentence. Each word will be used twice.

secret	private

1. Please go away! This is a _____ party and you were not invited.
2. The website is asking me to enter my _____ password.
3. We found a _____ passage in the old house, hidden in the kitchen.
4. Henry has always been a _____ person who keeps to himself.

B. Circle the word that relates best with each statement.

1. Mom did not tell anyone that she bought Dad a fishing rod for Father's Day.

   a. secret   b. private

2. This restaurant is only open to people who live in the building.

   a. secret   b. private

3. This is not public land, and you cannot walk across it.

   a. secret   b. private

Challenge Words

Check (✔) the words you already know.

☐ anonymous   ☐ personal   ☐ privacy   ☐ secrecy

271. Light

Check (✔) the words you already know. Then, listen and repeat.

 Tracks 1–5

☐ **bright**

TR 1

Definitions

Bright light is light that shines strongly.

A **clear** sky has no clouds.

If it is **light**, the sun is providing light from the beginning to the end of the day.

A **shiny** surface is bright and reflects light.

Sunshine is the light and heat that comes from the sun.

☐ **clear**

TR 2

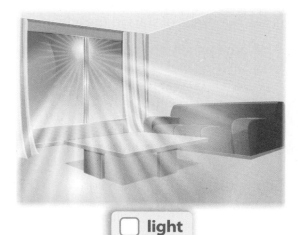

☐ **light**

TR 3

☐ **shiny**

TR 4

☐ **sunshine**

TR 5

Check Your Understanding

A. Match each word to the correct description. One description will not be used.

1. _____ bright
2. _____ clear
3. _____ light
4. _____ shiny
5. _____ sunshine

a. something that reflects light off its surface

b. the time of day when the sun is shining

c. heat and light produced by the sun

d. light produced by the moon

e. a sky without clouds

f. a light that shines strongly

B. Underline the correct word to complete each sentence.

1. Ray's (**light / shiny**) car looked new, but it was almost six years old.

2. The (**bright / sunshine**) light hurt my eyes when I looked up at it.

3. It gets (**shiny / light**) around six o'clock in the morning.

4. I saw hundreds of stars in the (**clear / shiny**) sky last night.

5. The large panels on top of the house use (**sunshine / clear**) to make energy for the home.

Challenge Words

Check (✔) the words you already know.

☐ brightness   ☐ daylight   ☐ luster   ☐ radiant

☐ brilliant   ☐ glimmer   ☐ moonlight   ☐ vivid

272. Light Producers

Check (✔) the words you already know. Then, listen and repeat.

 Tracks 1–5

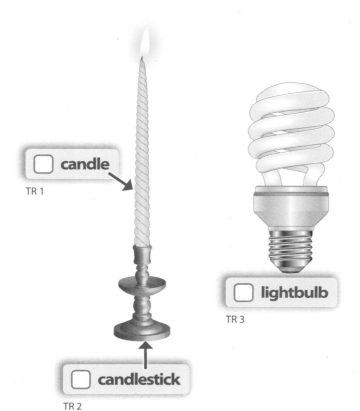

☐ **candle**
TR 1

☐ **candlestick**
TR 2

☐ **lightbulb**
TR 3

Definitions

A **candle** is a long stick of wax with a piece of string through the middle that you burn to give light.

A **candlestick** is a narrow object with a hole at the top that holds a candle.

A **lamp** is a light that works by using electricity or by burning oil or gas.

A **light** is an electric lamp that produces light.

A **lightbulb** is the circular glass part of an electric light.

☐ **lamp**
TR 4

☐ **light**
TR 5

Check Your Understanding

A. Choose the correct word from the word bank to complete each sentence.

candles	candlesticks	lamp	lights	lightbulb

1. Patricia is on the ladder, changing the _____ in the ceiling light.

2. Rosie has six _____ on her birthday cake.

3. The candles were placed in silver _____ on the dining table.

4. Flip this switch to turn off the _____ when you leave.

5. The _____ on Amy's desk is so beautiful. Does it give much light?

B. Circle the correct answer.

1. What does a candle look like?
   a. It is long and thin, with a small string coming out of it.
   b. It is a long piece of metal with a hole at the top of it.
   c. It is glass with a metal base that screws into a lamp.
2. What does a candlestick do?
   a. It gives off light.
   b. It holds a candle.
   c. It makes everything dark.
3. Where would you put a lightbulb?
   a. You put it into a lamp.
   b. You put it into a candle.
   c. You put it into a candlestick.
4. Where are the lights in your classroom?
   a. They are on the floor.
   b. They are on the door.
   c. They are on the ceiling.
5. What makes a lamp work?
   a. wood or gas
   b. electricity or oil
   c. *a* and *b*

Challenge Words

Check (✔) the words you already know.

- [ ] beacon
- [ ] beam
- [ ] flare
- [ ] fluorescent
- [ ] laser
- [ ] ray
- [ ] searchlight
- [ ] torch

306. Dark

Check (✔) the words you already know. Then, listen and repeat.

Tracks 1–3

☐ **shadow**

TR 1

Definitions

A **dark** room or place has little or no light.

Shade is an area where direct sunlight does not reach.

A **shadow** is a dark shape on a surface that is made when something blocks the light.

☐ **dark**

TR 2

☐ **shade**

TR 3

Check Your Understanding

A. Choose the correct word from the word bank to complete each sentence.

dark	shade	shadow

1. On the sunny day, the woman could see her _____ as she walked down the street.

2. I couldn't see anything in the _____ hallway, so I turned on the lights.

3. What a hot day! Let's get out of the sun and go sit in the _____ .

B. Write **T** for **true statements** and **F** for **false statements**.

1. _____ When you want it to be dark, you turn the lights on.

2. _____ If you see your shadow, you see a dark shape of your body.

3. _____ The sun makes you very hot when you are sitting in the shade.

4. _____ A dark room is very bright and sunny.

5. _____ People stay in the shade by sitting under a tree or an umbrella.

Challenge Words

Check (✔) the words you already know.

☐ blot   ☐ darkness   ☐ gloom   ☐ shady

☐ blur   ☐ fade   ☐ haze   ☐ splotch

58 LIGHT AND DARKNESS

372. Actions Related to Light

Check (✔) the words you already know. Then, listen and repeat.

Tracks 1–3

| reflect

TR 1

Definitions

To **reflect** means to give off a shine.

To **shine** means to give off light.

To **twinkle** means to give off light that is bright and then weak.

| shine

TR 2

| twinkle

TR 3

283

Check Your Understanding

A. Choose the correct word from the word bank to complete each sentence. Use each word once.

reflected	shines	twinkle

1. The stars _____ in the dark.

2. The car _____ the bright light, so I put on my sunglasses.

3. When the sun _____ very brightly, it is good to wear a hat.

B. Match each word to the correct description. One description will not be used.

1. _____ reflect

2. _____ shine

3. _____ twinkle

    a. become brighter and brighter

    b. give off bright light

    c. give off a shine

    d. quickly get bright and then dark again

Challenge Words

Check (✔) the words you already know.

- ☐ brighten
- ☐ flash
- ☐ glisten
- ☐ glitter
- ☐ glow
- ☐ illuminate
- ☐ lighten
- ☐ radiate
- ☐ shimmer
- ☐ sparkle

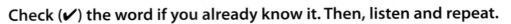

405. Clarity

Check (✔) the word if you already know it. Then, listen and repeat.

Track 1

TR 1

☐ invisible

Definition

If something is **invisible**, you cannot see it.

Check Your Understanding

A. Circle the correct answer.

1. Which of the following is *not* invisible?

   a. air   b. scents   c. clothes

2. Why might you feel invisible in a certain situation?

   a. People are ignoring you.   b. Everyone is talking to you.   c. You cannot see anything.

3. Why might you want to be invisible?

   a. You are meeting with friends.   b. You score the winning   c. You did something
                                            point in a game.   embarrassing.

B. Write **T** for **true statements** and **F** for **false statements**.

1. _____ An object that you can see is invisible.

2. _____ The sound that travels from an object to your ear is invisible.

3. _____ People can become invisible whenever they want to.

4. _____ People can only become invisible in books or stories.

5. _____ If you are invisible, you cannot see anything.

Challenge Words

Check (✔) the words you already know.

☐ clarity   ☐ dull   ☐ murky   ☐ transparent   ☐ visible

☐ dim   ☐ faint   ☐ pale   ☐ vague

262. Order and Complexity

Check (✔) the words you already know. Then, listen and repeat.

 Tracks 1–6

☐ **simple**
TR 1

☐ **blank**
TR 2

☐ **order**
TR 3

Check Your Understanding

A. Match each word to the correct description. One description will not be used.

1. _____ balance
2. _____ blank
3. _____ fancy
4. _____ order
5. _____ plain
6. _____ simple

a. everything in its place

b. having the basics, but nothing more

c. simple in style

d. elegant and detailed

e. a path-like puzzle that is difficult to solve

f. having different things be equally important

g. having no writing, marks, or decoration

Definitions

Balance means all of the different parts of something have the same importance.

Something that is **blank** has nothing on it.

Something that is **fancy** is elegant or detailed and is not simple or ordinary.

Order means that everything is in the correct place or happens at the correct time.

Something that is **plain** is very simple in style.

When something is **simple**, it has all the basic things it needs, but nothing more.

B. Underline the correct word to complete each sentence.

1. Are you going to leave this room looking so (**plain / fancy**)? Maybe you should hang some pictures.

2. If you are not sure how to answer question three, leave it (**blank / order**) and ask your teacher for help.

3. This meal is really quite (**simple / order**), but it tastes delicious.

4. For his graduation, Ed's grandparents took him to a (**fancy / blank**) restaurant.

5. Vera has been able to find a good (**plain / balance**) between work and school.

6. George wants more (**order / balance**) in his house, but his roommates are very messy.

Challenge Words

Check (✔) the words you already know.

- ☐ bleak
- ☐ complex
- ☐ elaborate
- ☐ equilibrium
- ☐ intricate
- ☐ maze
- ☐ neutral
- ☐ ornate
- ☐ turmoil
- ☐ void

290. Conformity to a Norm

Check (✔) the words you already know. Then, listen and repeat.

Tracks 1–5

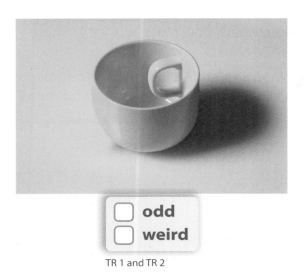

◻ **odd**
◻ **weird**

TR 1 and TR 2

◻ **rare**

TR 3

Check Your Understanding

A. Underline the correct word to complete each sentence.

1. There are very few of these birds in North America. It is very (**rare** / **weird**) to see one.

2. It is (**special** / **odd**) that Phillip hasn't called. I hope everything is all right.

3. I think it's a little (**weird** / **special**), but Rochelle likes to watch the same movie every Friday.

4. Is there a (**special** / **strange**) event today? Why are the children out of school?

5. It seems (**strange** / **rare**) that nobody is in class right now. Maybe they are in the library.

☐ **special**

TR 4

☐ **strange**

TR 5

Definitions

When someone or something is **odd**, that person or thing is strange or unusual.

Something that is **rare** is not seen or heard very often or does not happen often.

Someone or something that is **special** is different from what is normal or usual.

Something that is **strange** is unusual or unexpected.

When something or someone is **weird**, that thing or person is strange.

B. Write **T** for **true statements** and **F** for **false statements**.

1. _____ It is odd to go home after school if there is nothing else to do.

2. _____ A rare coin might be worth a lot of money.

3. _____ If you wear a special outfit to school, it is what you wear on most days.

4. _____ It would be strange to see a frog with three legs.

5. _____ If your best friend stops talking to you without saying why, you might think that she is acting weird.

Challenge Words

Check (✔) the words you already know.

☐ bizarre   ☐ eccentric   ☐ peculiar   ☐ uncommon

☐ distinct   ☐ original   ☐ uncanny   ☐ unique

377. Chemicals

Check (✔) the words you already know. Then, listen and repeat.

Tracks 1–3

☐ **oxygen**

TR 1

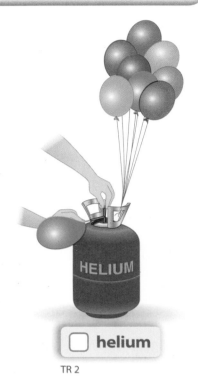

☐ **helium**

TR 2

Check Your Understanding

A. Write **T** for **true statements** and **F** for **false statements**.

1. _____ After you drink something with oxygen, you feel more awake.

2. _____ After you drink something with caffeine, you feel more awake.

3. _____ Your body depends on helium to survive.

4. _____ Helium is used to make balloons float.

5. _____ Tea and coffee both have caffeine in them.

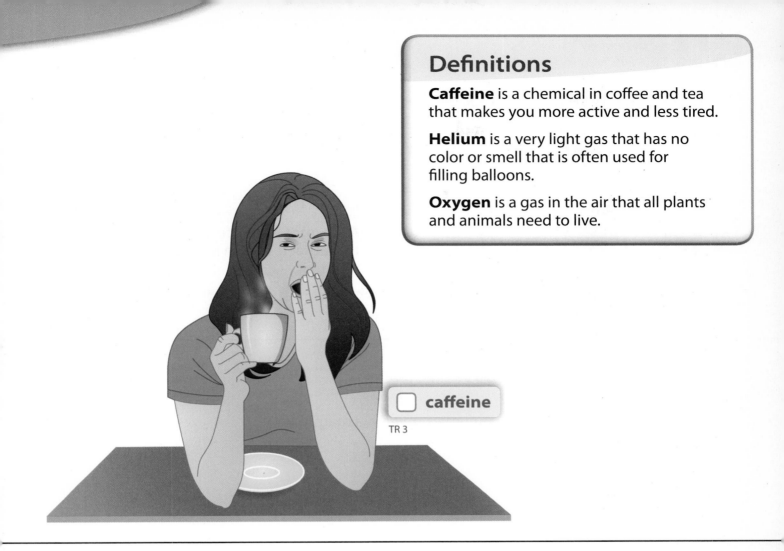

Definitions

Caffeine is a chemical in coffee and tea that makes you more active and less tired.

Helium is a very light gas that has no color or smell that is often used for filling balloons.

Oxygen is a gas in the air that all plants and animals need to live.

☐ **caffeine**

TR 3

B. Match each chemical to the item that contains it.

1. _____ caffeine

2. _____ helium

3. _____ oxygen

a. the air you breathe

b. a cup of tea

c. a balloon

Challenge Words

Check (✔) the words you already know.

☐ chemical   ☐ cholesterol   ☐ compound

418. Electricity and Magnetism

Check (✔) the word if you already know it. Then, listen and repeat.

Track 1

☐ **magnet**
TR 1

Definition

A **magnet** is a piece of special metal that attracts certain metals, such as iron, toward it.

Check Your Understanding

A. Check (✔) the items that you could pick up with a **magnet**.

☐ an apple

☐ a paper clip

☐ a book

☐ a key

☐ a coin

B. Write **T** for **true statements** and **F** for **false statements**.

1. _____ A magnet attracts other metals to it.

2. _____ A magnet attracts wood or plastic to it.

3. _____ A magnet can hold any two objects together.

4. _____ Many people like to decorate their refrigerators with magnets.

Challenge Words

Check (✔) the words you already know.

☐ charge   ☐ hydroelectric   ☐ radiation

☐ electric   ☐ microwave   ☐ radioactive

APPENDIX

295

Note: This Appendix provides information on how to find each cluster. To locate a specific <u>super cluster</u>, please refer to the Contents on pages v to vi.